Getting Your Kid on a Gluten-Free Casein-Free Diet

of related interest

Dietary Interventions in Autism Spectrum Disorders
Why They Work Why They Do, Why They Don't When They Don't
Ken Aitken
ISBN 978 1 84310 939 6

A User Guide to the GF/CF Diet for Autism,
Asperger Syndrome and AD/HD
Luke Jackson
Foreword by Marilyn Le Breton
ISBN 978 1 84310 055 3

Autism and Diet
What You Need to Know
Rosemary Kessick
ISBN 978 1 84310 983 9

Autism and Gastrointestinal Complaints
What You Need to Know
Rosemary Kessick
ISBN 978 1 84310 984 6

Diet Intervention and Autism
Implementing the Gluten Free and Casein Free Diet for Autistic
Children and Adults – A Practical Guide for Parents
Marilyn Le Breton
Foreword by Rosemary Kessick, Allergy Induced Autism
ISBN 978 1 85302 935 6

Getting Your Kid on a Gluten-Free Casein-Free Diet

Susan Lord

Jessica Kingsley Publishers
London and Philadelphia

LSTA Autism Grant

Every effort has been made to ensure that the information contained in this book is correct. Please check carefully through every recipe used to make sure that it is suitable for whom it is intended. Neither the author nor the publisher takes any responsibility for any consequences of any decision made as a result of the information contained in this book.

The author does not endorse, approve, or assume responsibility for any recipe, product, brand or company. The presence (or absence) of a product does not constitute approval (or disapproval) by the author.

Nothing in this book is to be substituted for medical advice. Readers are encouraged to consult a physician regarding treatment of their medical problems. Always consult a qualified medical practitioner before implementing any dietary intervention.

First published in 2009
by Jessica Kingsley Publishers
116 Pentonville Road
London N1 9JB, UK
and
400 Market Street, Suite 400
Philadelphia, PA 19106, USA

www.jkp.com

Copyright © Susan Lord 2009

Library of Congress Cataloging in Publication Data
A CIP catalog record for this book is available from the Library of Congress

British Library Cataloguing in Publication Data
A CIP catalogue record for this book is available from the British Library

ISBN 978 1 84310 909 9

Printed and bound in Great Britain by
Athenaeum Press, Gateshead, Tyne and Wear

To Jenny, my grounding earth —
and Christine, my shooting star.
To my husband Dan, for believing in me.
To my parents, Bill and Joyce,
for giving me the world.

Contents

Part III The Cookbook

Acknowledgements

To Dr. Mary Megson, MD, of Richmond, Virginia, USA, who gave me the nudge I needed to start Jenny on the Gluten-Free Casein-Free Diet, and thus begin our journey, never to return.

I am grateful for the teachers in my past for selflessly sharing their knowledge so that this book could be possible. Thank you to Bill Maffie, Fred Jewitt, George Murphy and Meg Gallagher of the Hingham Public School system in Hingham Massachusetts, USA, for coaxing the writer out of me.

To those who believed in me and encouraged me the whole way. To Melba Felty, who listened to a dream in its infancy; to Amy Whorf McGiggan, for the inspiration on the beach that got me re-energized to submit this book proposal; and to Deborah Goldthwaite, for her prayers and unending encouragement. To Steve Nelson, for his advice on sticking with a project that's worth the time and the effort it takes to see it to completion. To Lynn Halsey, for gently convincing me that ownership of work is limiting and, by giving it up, the Universe can gain a whole lot more.

To Beth and Jim Whelan, for helping me test recipes in their kitchen and for learning this diet along the way with me.

To Karyn Seroussi and Lisa Lewis, for providing the first books available on the subject. And to Bette Hagman, the pioneer.

I thank my husband for bringing me food and coffee as I typed away in the basement, to meet this deadline. To my kids, for believing that their mom was a published author way before she ever was. And to my parents, for convincing me I could be anything I wanted to be.

Introduction

This hit home for me: I think it will for you, too.

Welcome to Holland

I am often asked to describe the experience of raising a child with a disability – to try to help people who have not shared that unique experience to understand it, to imagine how it would feel.

It's like this...

When you're going to have a baby, it's like planning a fabulous vacation trip – to Italy. You buy a bunch of guide books and make wonderful plans. The Coliseum. The Michelangelo David. The gondolas in Venice. You may learn some handy phrases in Italian. It's all very exciting. After months of eager anticipation, the day finally arrives. You pack your bags and off you go. Several hours later, the plane lands. The stewardess comes in and says, "Welcome to Holland." "Holland?!?" you say. "What do you mean Holland?? I signed up for Italy! I'm supposed to be in Italy. All my life I've dreamed of going to Italy."

But there's been a change in the flight plan. They've landed in Holland and there you must stay. The important thing is they haven't taken you to a horrible, disgusting, filthy place full of pestilence, famine and disease. It's just a different place.

So you must go out and buy new guide books. And you must learn a whole new language. And you will meet a whole new group of people you would never have met.

It's just a different place. It's slower-paced than Italy, less flashy than Italy. But after you've been there for a while and you catch your breath, you look around…and you begin to notice Holland has windmills…and Holland has tulips. Holland even has Rembrandts.

But everyone you know is busy coming and going from Italy…and they're bragging about what a wonderful time they had there. And for the rest of your life, you will say, "Yes, that's where I was supposed to go. That's what I had planned."

And the pain of that will never, ever, ever, ever go away…because the loss of that dream is a very very significant loss.

But, if you spend your life mourning the fact that you didn't get to Italy, you may never be free to enjoy the very special, the very lovely things…about Holland.

My father's words echo in my head, "I never told you life was gonna be easy, Susie."

Having grown up with a severely retarded brother with Down Syndrome, my plane was routed to Holland at the tender age of three. Catapult myself 27 years in the future, I am pregnant with my first child, Jenny, my bags are packed for Italy. I had done my time in Holland already. I was exempt. When Jenny was born, she didn't cry. It was an eerie silence and I knew I had landed in Holland…again, forever.

I had planned to have four kids, all boys, and they would all be smart, handsome and athletic. They would attend Ivy League schools and drive Mercedes Benzes off into the sunset with their beautiful wives. My work would then be done.

Well, reality is that I have two girls. I never did leave Holland as expected. I never got to Italy as planned. I must admit, I have learned many valuable lessons in Holland. At first I didn't see the windmills or the tulips, but now I do. I learned to bloom where planted – I am planted in Holland, blooming more beautifully with each spring.

Loving your child means not being sure and not knowing what comes next. It's all about guesswork, trusting your instincts and having lots of faith.

My childless neighbor asked me, "Is that your baby?" referring to my second daughter. I replied, "Yes, can you believe it?" For me, an eternity had passed: from breastfeeding and diapers, to potty trained with a teenager's attitude. To him, merely three short years in his never-changing life had slipped away.

My life has been so enriched by my children, and it is not my youngest daughter that I write about in this book: my 14-year-old daughter, Jenny, is the inspiration for these words. Jenny was diagnosed with Autistic Spectrum Disorder (ASD) at the age of five, after countless visits to pediatricians, neurologists and specialists. If you are reading this, you probably have a child with developmental difficulty and know how slowly time can snail as you await a diagnosis, or perhaps deny that one exists at all. I am so thankful for this diagnosis, because now, I can help her to be the best she can be. I truly believe that Jenny has progressed so wonderfully because of the major changes in her diet. If you are considering starting a gluten-free casein-free (GFCF) diet or you have started the diet and are looking for it to be easier, read on!

Without children, there is no time. With typical children, time exists. With special needs children, every second is precious. Don't delay.

This book is a step-by-step tool to guide you as you remove the proteins casein and gluten from your child's diet. It is designed to give you simple, practical, easy-to-understand guidance in beginning the diet and sound nutritional advice on how to do it right, so that it can help your child and not harm him. I want you to move on past the lame excuse, "When I checked with his doctor, he said that he'd seen more kids harmed by poor nutrition from the diet than helped by the diet."

We will approach it in three gradual steps:

1. Nutrition first.

2. Remove casein.

3. Remove gluten.

Note: To aid clarity 'he' is used throughout when reference is made to a child.

PART I

The Gluten-Free
Casein-Free Diet

CHAPTER 1

Nutrition First

Step 1: Nutrition first

Good nutrition is essential for everyone, especially children. With compromised nutrition, we risk stunted growth, delayed development, sickness and disease. The goal is to find nutrition in food first and then supplement for added insurance. This chapter will focus on essential nutrients, vitamins and minerals and those foods that offer more "bang for your buck," nutritionally speaking. We will also discuss proper supplementation.

Generally, a child should have three meals and two snacks per day. Meals should consist of one or two servings of grain (like corn tortillas, or GF bread, rice or GF pasta), one or two servings of vegetables, a serving of fruit, 1–3 oz (25–75g) of lean meat, and a calcium-fortified soy or rice yogurt or beverage (USDA 2005b). Remember that a child needs to drink plenty of fluids, preferably water. Juice and soy, rice or potato milk are also good choices. Absolutely limit soda, sweet sugary drinks, or any kind of juice imposter that is not 100 percent pure fruit juice. Most importantly, make sure that everyone in the family gets at least five servings of fruits and vegetables every day. I can not stress how important this is for overall health and well being, as well as for disease prevention.

Serving sizes will vary according to age, activity level and growth pattern. Follow the general guide in Tables 1.1 and 1.2 for recommended number of servings per food group and amounts of food per serving size. Trust your child's internal mechanism of hunger. If he is hungry, he will eat. If not, he won't. Don't freak out if a child does not eat much at any given meal or snack. It is not a reflection of your parenting abilities if the child is simply not hungry! Let it go…he will eat well again very soon. If a child is trained to eat when not hungry, out of habit, because of a strict time schedule or out of boredom, he will take in too many calories and become overweight, setting up poor eating behaviors for the rest of his life.

Table 1.1 Serving sizes for children to age six

Food group	Serving sizes for age/height		
Alternative dairy group Include 3–4 servings daily of the following foods	1–2 years 29"–34" tall	2–3 years 34"–37" tall	3–6 years 37"–45" tall
Non-dairy calcium and vitamin D fortified milk	½ cup	½–⅓ cup	¾ cup
CF non-dairy cheese	1 oz (25g)	1 oz (25g)	1 oz (25g)
CF non-dairy yogurt	¼ cup	¼ cup	¼ cup
CF non-dairy ice cream	½ cup	½ cup	½ cup
CF non-dairy pudding	½ cup	¾ cup	¾ cup
Meat group Include 2 or more servings daily of the following foods	1–2 years 29"–34" tall	2–3 years 34"–37" tall	3–6 years 37"–45" tall
Meat, fish, chicken, turkey	1 oz (25g)	1–2 oz (25–50g)	1.5–2 oz (40–50g)
Eggs	1	1	1
Peanut butter	none	none	3 tbsp
CF non-dairy cheese	1 oz (25g)	1 oz (25g)	1 oz (25g)

Dried beans and peas	¼ cup	¼ cup	¼ cup
Food group	**Serving sizes for age/height**		
Bread and cereal group Include 6 or more servings daily of the following foods	**1–2 years 29"–34" tall**	**2–3 years 34"–37" tall**	**3–6 years 37"–45" tall**
Enriched GFCF bread	½ slice	½ slice	1 slice
Ready-to-eat GFCF cereal	¼ cup	⅓ cup	½ cup
Cooked GFCF cereal	2 tbsp	2 tbsp	¼ cup
GFCF crackers	3	3	5
Fruit and vegetable group Include 5 or more servings daily of the following foods	**1–2 years 29"–34" tall**	**2–3 years 34"–37" tall**	**3–6 years 37"–45" tall**
Unsweetened fruit juice	¼–½ cup	½ cup	½ cup
Citrus fruit, berries, tomato, cabbage	¼ cup	¼ cup	½ cup
Other fruits (fresh, or canned)	2 tbsp	2 tbsp	2 tbsp
Green vegetables (broccoli, spinach)	2 tbsp	2 tbsp	2 tbsp
Orange vegetables (squash, carrots, etc.)	2 tbsp	2 tbsp	2 tbsp
Other vegetables (potato, corn)	2 tbsp	2 tbsp	2 tbsp

Source: USDA 2005b

After age six, serving sizes will be comparable to adult serving sizes listed in Table 1.2.

Table 1.2 Serving sizes for children age six and up

Food group	Serving sizes for children age 6 and up
Alternative dairy group Include 3–4 servings daily of the following foods	
Non-dairy calcium and vitamin D fortified milk	1 cup
CF non-dairy cheese	2 slices
CF non-dairy yogurt	1 cup
CF non-dairy ice cream	1½ cups
CF non-dairy pudding	1½ cups
Meat group Include 2 or more servings daily of the following foods	
Meat, fish, chicken, turkey	2 oz (50g)
Eggs	2
Peanut butter	4 tbsp
CF non-dairy cheese	2 oz (50g)
Dried beans and peas	1 cup cooked
Bread and cereal group Include 6 or more servings daily of the following foods	
Enriched GFCF bread	1 slice
Ready-to-eat GFCF cereal	¾–1 cup
Cooked GFCF cereal	½ cup
GFCF crackers	5

Food group	Serving sizes for children age 6 and up
Fruit and vegetable group Include 5 or more servings daily of the following foods	
Unsweetened fruit juice	¾ cup
Citrus fruit, berries, tomato, cabbage	1 cup – fresh raw
Other fruits (canned)	½ cup
Green vegetables (broccoli, spinach)	½ cup cooked, 1 cup raw
Orange vegetables (squash, carrots, etc.)	½ cup cooked, 1 cup raw
Other vegetables (potato, corn)	½ cup

Source: USDA 2005b

The meals, snack items, menus and recipes in this guide book are designed with good nutrition in mind. Our goal is to be efficient when we eat, choosing wisely and in good combination to maximize nutrition from appropriate amounts of food and calories. This may not always be possible on a day-to-day basis, given the crazy busy lives that we lead. Just for extra insurance, we will complete the optimum daily intake with a multivitamin and mineral supplement.

Fortunately, there are many excellent supplements on the market. Supplementation is very important in this process and should be started about two weeks before the removal of the proteins casein and gluten from the diet.

Goal

To supplement essential vitamins and minerals that could be lost when altering the child's diet.

Why

To take casein out of the diet, we must take dairy products out of the diet. To take dairy out of the child's diet means taking a huge source of calcium and vitamin D away. Calcium is an essential mineral needed for healthy teeth and bones, for nerves to send their messages, for muscles to do their work, for the heart to beat, for blood to clot and for a healthy immune system. Calcium deficiency in children can cause bone deformities and slow growth. Later in life, not getting enough calcium can lead to osteoporosis, high blood pressure, and certain types of cancer. This would not be a responsible thing to do without substituting other foods like calcium and vitamin D fortified soy milk and/or yogurt, and without the extra insurance of adding a daily multivitamin and mineral supplement.

To live gluten-free, we must remove many grain products from the diet: anything made with wheat, barley, or oats to name a few. B vitamins – specifically, thiamin, riboflavin, niacin, B6, folic acid and B12 which are important for normal growth and development, among other things – would be lost unless replaced by fortified gluten-free foods and daily supplementation.

How

I recommend a GFCF multivitamin and mineral supplement, which will provide essential nutrients lost by removing dairy foods and certain grain products from the diet. There are so many vitamin and mineral supplements on the market, it is overwhelming to have to make a decision regarding which one to buy. How do you know which one to choose? First, if your child is younger than 12 years old, make sure that the supplement is especially made for children. Over 12 years of age, you may buy an adult formula. If your child is not getting at least 16 oz of non-dairy milk or yogurt that is fortified with calcium and vitamin D, you will want to choose a multivitamin with added calcium. If your child is not a big meat eater, and is not getting the recommended serving sizes of the meat group, you will want to supplement with a multivitamin with added iron. If neither milk alternatives nor meat are a challenge, just a simple daily multivitamin is recommended.

CHAPTER 2

Going Casein-Free

Step 2: Remove casein

Goal

To remove the protein casein from the child's diet.

Why

There are two schools of thought.

These beautiful, bright kids have developmentally challenged intestines, and:

1. they are more likely to have food allergies, sensitivities or intolerances. (D'Eufemia *et al.* 1996; Horvath *et al.* 1999) or

2. certain proteins (the ones in milk and wheat) are broken down to produce chemicals that mimic morphine in their little bodies, thus causing a "drugged" effect. (Reichelt *et al.* 1990; Shattock *et al.* 1990).

My daughter, Jenny, tested positive for an allergy to casein, the protein in milk. For her, quite simply, if the food item has casein in it, she is better off without it. We explain it to others like this: "Jenny can't have that [ice cream, milk, cookie, whatever] because it will make her sick and take her words away."

How

The protein casein is found in all dairy products and also in some processed foods. Milk, cheese, yogurt and butter are the biggest sources, but crackers, animal cookies, cream sauces, cheese sauces and soups can contain casein too.

Basically, you must read every label of every food you plan to feed your child. And here is a list of ingredients that will cause you to put the food item back on the shelf:

- ○ Milk
- ○ Skim milk
- ○ Butter
- ○ Yogurt
- ○ Lactose
- ○ Powdered milk
- ○ Goat's milk
- ○ Cheese
- ○ Casein
- ○ Caseinate or caseinates
- ○ Whey.

Finding alternatives for milk, yogurt, ice cream, butter and cheese went smoothly; in fact there are a variety of foods to choose from as substitutes. Table 2.1 will give you a few ideas to get started.

After completely removing casein, the offending dairy protein, from your child's diet, it usually takes three days to three weeks for the child's body to rid itself of the casomorphine and during this time you may even see a regression in behavior. For example, any of the characteristic "autistic" behavior that your child exhibited will be heightened in this time frame. Do not panic! You should actually be encouraged by this regression; this is a good sign and is referred to as the "die off" period. It is as though he is going through "withdrawal" from this drug. After the withdrawal, you should see progress (Knivsberg *et al.* 1990, 1994; Reichelt *et al.* 1990). Progress in the form of more speech, better eye contact, less

Table 2.1 Dairy alternatives

Instead of	Choose
Milk	Soy milk or Rice milk – there are a variety of wonderful soy milks and rice milks on the shelf and in the dairy case. They are tasty, some are flavored, and will serve you well in any recipe that calls for milk. Remember to always read the label!
Powdered milk	Vance's brand Dari-Free (order over the internet) Soy infant formula
Butter	Soy butter spread – tastes good and no trans-fats! Remember that trans-fats are NOT healthy for our bodies!
Yogurt	Soy yogurt (for example, The WholeSoy Company – www.wholesoy.com or 1–415–495–2870 – WholeSoy creamy cultured soy yogurt is available in many flavors)
Cheese	Soy cheese (for example, Vegan Soymage products www.galaxyfoods.com or 1–407–855–6600)
Cream sauce	Non-dairy cream sauce (for example, Pacific foods non-dairy cream sauce – available at Whole Foods Market 1–503–692–9666)
Ice cream	Soy, tofu or rice based frozen desserts; Sorbet; Fruit bars
Cream cheese	Tofu-based cream cheese (for example "Better than Cream Cheese" available at whole foods market)
Sour cream	Plain flavored soy yogurt

tantrums, less screaming, better sleep patterns, more social behavior, less "stimming" (self-stimulatory behavior, like flapping of arms, spinning wheels on toy trucks, or repetitive speech patterns) and less self-injurious behavior (SIB). You may want to stop here and hang out for a while to catch your breath. I would recommend giving this phase a full three weeks before moving on to remove gluten. And then, I assure you, when you get your courage up again and proceed on to remove gluten, you will see yet another set of doors open for your very special child.

CHAPTER 3

Going Gluten-Free

Step 3: Remove gluten

Removing casein from Jenny's diet was not hard. She adjusted well and lots of people have a "lactose intolerance," so it wasn't a big deal when I had to explain to others that Jenny could not have milk or cheese. On the other hand, just the thought of removing gluten overwhelmed me. I wondered how I would possibly accomplish that. Our gluten-free casein-free journey has added a whole new dimension to our family life. A dimension that has challenged us but that we have met head on with a robust sense of humor, and a new appreciation for accepting ourselves just the way we are right now.

I assure you, if you think you can not do it, I know you can! Take it from someone who has never taken a home-economics class, whose kitchen is 10 feet by 12 feet (no lie), and whose perfectionist qualities would prevent her from attempting the simplest of tasks for fear of failure. My blood pressure goes up just watching those cooking shows on the food network!

I have eaten my fair share of pasta, believe me, but I have never made pasta from scratch, let alone gluten-free pasta, in a brand-new, never-been-used pasta maker. The feeling of inadequacy welled up inside me: never good enough. Uncomfortable feelings, "you are a failure" feelings. In the middle of the process, when the skinny spaghetti stands were sticking together to make one big fat cord of gluten-less mess, I wanted to throw the dough *and* the pasta maker in the trash. The noodles were too sticky, my hands were webbed with dough and no amount of potato starch flour would help. I was extremely frustrated. But this time, because it was nourishment for my beloved child, I did not quit like the many times before, when I felt those familiar feelings of inadequacy. I was going to make this work. My baby would have spaghetti at our church supper just like everyone else! I was motivated by a passion for the cause that made me forge onward. I separated the strands from the cord as best I could and boiled that salted water. I plunged the spaghetti into the rolling oiled boil and about 9 minutes later, I had a slightly less than perfect product that tasted like a dish from the Italian "North-End" in Boston. It was absolutely delicious and Jenny loved it. She ate all four servings in one sitting. Seeing her enjoying her homemade pasta made me so proud, it was worth all the frustration, all the uncomfortable "I am a failure" feelings. So, when you are feeling inadequate as a GFCF chef, forge onward, because the outcome may not be as bad as you expect it to be. You may be pleasantly surprised. Through my special child, I have learned so much about life, love and my own self. When it comes to my kid and the progress she is making, I am learning to accept less than perfect from her, from me, and from my spaghetti. And that is the best gift I could ever give her and the best gift I have ever received.

Getting rid of gluten

Gluten is the generic name for certain types of proteins contained in the common cereal grains wheat, rye, barley, and possibly oats.

The grains that are NOT allowed in any form on the gluten free diet are listed below.

When reading labels, you want to AVOID any product that contains these ingredients:

- Wheat (durum, semolina, kamut, spelt)
- Rye
- Barley
- Triticale
- Oats.

The grains that are ALLOWED on a gluten-free diet are:
- Rice
- Corn
- Soy
- Potato
- Tapioca
- Beans
- Sorghum
- Quinoa
- Millet
- Buckwheat
- Arrowroot
- Amaranth
- Tef
- Nut flours.

Foods that often contain gluten are listed below and are to be AVOIDED as well:
- Breading
- Broth
- Coating mixes
- Communion wafers
- Croutons
- Imitation bacon
- Imitation seafood
- Marinades
- Pastas
- Processed meats
- Roux
- Sauces
- Self-basting poultry
- Soup bases
- Stuffings
- Thickeners.

The key to following a gluten-free diet is to become a good label reader. Listed below are questionable ingredients – these ingredients should be avoided unless you can verify that they do not contain gluten:

- Brown rice syrup (frequently made from barley)
- Caramel color
- Dextrin (usually a corn-based product but may be derived from wheat)
- Flour
- Cereal products
- Hydrolyzed vegetable protein (HVP)
- Vegetable protein or hydrolyzed plant protein (HPP)
- Textured vegetable protein (TVP)
- Malt or malt flavoring (usually made from barley)
- Malt vinegar
- Modified food starch
- Mono- and di-glycerides (in dry products only)
- Flavorings in meat products
- Soy sauce
- Soy sauce solids
- Vegetable gum.

When you are not certain from a food label if the food is safe to consume on a GFCF diet, call the manufacturer and specify the ingredient and lot number of the food in question. State your needs clearly; be patient, persistent and polite.

Remember that wheat-free is not gluten-free. Wheat-free products may still contain rye, oats, barley or other ingredients that are not gluten-free.

The following chapters include sample meals and daily menus, complete with shopping lists. I have included recipes for you to follow in easy, step-by-step form. Remember to be an avid label reader and keep your pantry stocked with essential GFCF foods.

PART II

Gluten-Free Casein-Free Meals

CHAPTER 4

What's for Breakfast?

Breakfast is the most important meal of the day. Breakfast "breaks the fast" of the night's slumber. We have just slept for eight hours and have had nothing to eat, so we need to stoke up that furnace, put some wood on the fire, put some fuel in the tank. Breakfast does this for our body. Best case scenario, when you are starting out on this diet, is that you are home for most meals. As you get more used to the diet, it will be easier to go out to eat, but for now, as you get acclimated to this new way of life, cooking and eating at home is your best bet. This chapter will give you 14 breakfast ideas to get you through the first two weeks.

14 breakfast ideas

1. Waffles made from scratch (see recipe p.104) (or GFCF frozen waffles) with GFCF buttery spread

   100% pure maple syrup

   Calcium fortified soy milk

   Sliced fresh pears

2. Fried potatoes (see recipe p.105)

   Fruit juice

Pan fried ham

Fried egg

3. Breakfast coffee cake (see recipe p.103)

    Calcium fortified soy milk

4. GF bread toasted with jam or honey

    Calcium fortified soy milk

5. GFCF breakfast cereal with calcium fortified soy milk and a banana

6. Applesauce pancakes (see recipe p.101) with GFCF buttery spread

    100% pure maple syrup

    Calcium fortified soy milk

7. Blueberry muffins (see recipe p.102)

    Calcium fortified soy milk

8. GF French toast (see recipe p.100) with GFCF buttery spread and 100% pure maple syrup

    Pineapple juice

9. Boiled white rice with GFCF buttery spread melted on top a little brown sugar and a pinch of salt

    Fruit juice

10. Corn bread with GFCF buttery spread (see recipe p.157)

    Calcium fortified soy milk

11. Instant grits

    Calcium fortified soy milk

12. Applesauce bread (see recipe p.158)

    Calcium fortified soy milk

13. Bacon and eggs

    GFCF toast with GFCF buttery spread

    Calcium fortified soy milk

    Orange juice

14. Scrambled eggs and sausage

    Calcium fortified soy milk

    Sliced fresh apples

CHAPTER 5

Is It Lunch Time Yet?

Lunch replenishes mid day. Eating well at lunch will ensure that your child will have energy for the afternoon. Most kids tend to eat the most food at breakfast, less at lunch and even less at dinner. If this is true for your child, you may try switching some of the heartier dinner ideas to the lunch meal and moving the lighter lunch fare featured here, to dinner time, when little bodies are tired and cranky and not feeling so much like eating. This chapter provides you with 14 lunch ideas to get you through your first two weeks on the diet.

14 lunch ideas

1.   Peanut butter (or any nut butter) and jelly sandwich on GF bread (see recipe p.129)
     Cucumber slices
     Fruit juice

2.   Turkey and soy cheese sandwich on corn tortillas
     Pineapple chunks
     Water

3.   Ham and soy cheese sandwich on GF bread
     Carrot sticks
     Rice milk

4. Chicken sandwich (see recipe p.151) on GF bread
   GF potato chips
   Fruit juice

5. Tuna sandwich (see recipe p.152) on GF bread
   Canned pears
   Water

6. Egg sandwich (see recipe p.153) on GF bread
   White grapes
   Soy milk

7. Tortilla pizza (see recipe p.112)
   Garden salad
   Fruit juice

8. Hotdogs and baked beans
   Water

9. Red potato and chicken salad (see recipe p.117)
   Cherry tomatoes
   Water

10. Grilled chicken breast sandwich with lettuce and tomato on gluten-free bun
    Soy milk

11. Turkey chili in a can or made from scratch (see recipe p.131)
    Corn bread (see recipe p.157)
    Soy milk

12. Chicken nuggets (see recipe p.130)
    French fries
    Fruit juice

13. Fried rice (see recipe see p.135)
    Fruit Juice

14. Peanut butter and banana on a corn tortilla (see recipe
    p.128)
    Water

CHAPTER 6

Servin' Supper

Dinner is a time for the family to spend quality time together. Yeah, right. Dinner time in our household is the most hectic time of the day! Usually, it goes more like this: I am trying to get the meal on the table without burning something, myself included, at least one child is melting down or screaming, children are fighting, stainable liquid gets spilled all over the floor, and after I manage to get something on the table that resembles supper, the baby starts to cry right as I sit down to eat. Sound familiar? That is what dinner time is all about in the real world. Bon Appetit!

Here are 14 suggestions for the last meal of the day. As I mentioned in the last chapter, you may want to switch dinner with lunch to appease healthier appetites in the middle of the day.

14 dinner ideas

1. Meatloaf (see recipe p.111)

    Mashed potatoes made with rice milk and GFCF buttery spread

    Cooked carrots

    Soy milk

2. Sweet and sour stir fry (see recipe p.131)

White rice

Steamed sugar snap peas

Fruit juice

3. Citrus glazed salmon (see recipe p.122)

    Brown rice

    Summer squash

    Water

4. Grilled flank steak and mixed greens salad (see recipe p.119)

    Sweet rice (see recipe p.144)

    Calcium fortified soy milk

5. Scallops with ginger sauce (see recipe p.118)

    Baked sweet potatoes

    Fruit juice

6. Chili (see recipe p.132)

    White rice

    Soy milk

7. Pad Thai (see recipe p.115)

    Indian quick bread (see recipe p.161)

    Water

8. Southwestern stuffed acorn squash (see recipe p.121)

    Brown rice

    Calcium fortified soy milk

9. GFCF pizza – you can buy GF pizza shells in the freezer section of your natural food store or you can

make your own crust (see recipe p.134) Make sure you use CF cheese!

Potato chips

Fruit juice

10. Chicken and dumplins' (see recipe p.108)

    Steamed carrots

    Soy milk

11. Spaghetti and meatballs (see recipes pp.126 and 127)

    GF garlic bread (see recipe p.159)

    Rice milk

12. Hamburger patty on GF bun

    French fries

    Fruit juice

13. Chicken curry (see recipe p.116)

    Sliced cucumber

    Fruit juice

14. Baked whole chicken

    Baked potatoes

    Steamed broccoli

    Fruit juice

CHAPTER 7

Snacks

Snacks are the fillers that will get you out of tight spots throughout the day. By "tight spots," I mean those times when someone is about to "lose it" in a public place, usually a library where you are supposed to be quiet or the grocery store, when you have a cart full of your week's staples and you are entering the checkout line. Those times when everyone is staring at you like you are the only mother on earth who has kids that misbehave from time to time. Those times when you ask yourself, "Why did I think this motherhood thing was a good idea?" Before I had kids and *I* was the one doing the staring, I told myself that I would NEVER let my screaming child (not that I would ever *have* a screaming child) have a candy bar in the checkout line, just to shut her up. I told myself I would never open a box full of crackers or breakfast cereal in the store for my kid to eat before we paid for it. I told myself lots of things that have since taught me the valuable lesson called "never say never." Unfortunately, when your child is following a GFCF diet, it is much harder to get out of the tight spots without prior planning and forethought. Unfortunately, you can't just open a box of any crackers or cereal to placate your child who is about to make a scene in front of a bunch of childless "know-it-alls"! So you must plan for these times. This chapter gives you 30 snack ideas, many that travel well, keep in the car or can be stored in the invaluable Mommy-bag better known as a "purse."

30 snacks

1. Trail mix (see recipe p.162)

2. Potato chips

3. Air popped popcorn with salt and GFCF buttery spread melted and poured over it.

4. Loretta O's Peanut Butter Cookies (see recipe p.175)

5. Canned or fresh pineapple chunks

6. GFCF rice cakes

7. Sliced canned pears

8. Blueberry muffins (see recipe p.102)

9. Fresh grapes – frozen grapes are yummy!

10. Fresh pears

11. Waffles (see recipe p.104)

12. Banana

13. Peanuts

14. GF pretzels

15. Cashews

16. Applesauce

17. Kiwi fruit

18. Fresh apples

19. Macadamia nuts

20. Peanut butter and rice crackers

21. Macaroons

22. Canned peaches

23. Canned mandarin oranges

24. Fresh oranges

25. GFCF soy pudding (Brand: Zen Soy)

26. Banana chips

27. Ginger bread (see recipe p.156)

28. Sliced cucumbers

29. Marshmallow treats (see recipe p.171)

30. Fruit and popcorn bars (see recipe p.163)

CHAPTER 8

Delicious Desserts

Ah, dessert! My favorite meal of the day. Did I, the Registered Dietitian, say that? When you make these desserts in your own kitchen, as I have made them in mine, you will not even know that they are lacking regular wheat flour and/or milk from a cow. Enjoy!

6 desserts

1. Apple crisp (recipe p.167)

2. Dark fudge brownies (see recipe p.172)

3. GFCF soy or rice or tofu based "ice cream" – sold in the freezer section of most grocery stores

4. Peanut butter cookies (see recipe p.176)

5. Sugar cookies (see recipe p.173)

6. Chocolate chip cookies (see recipe p.177)

CHAPTER 9

Two Weeks
of Nutritionally
Balanced Menus

The menus in this chapter are based on all of the sound nutritional guidelines that have been outlined in the previous chapters. Following these daily meal plans will ensure that your child is getting the optimum nutrition that he needs. Each day and subsequently, each week is designed to give your child the necessary vitamins and minerals (including vitamin A, D and calcium) that he needs. Also, the number of servings of each food group (for example, grains, meats, and vegetables) is carefully calculated for each day. If your child is eating five or more servings of fruits and vegetables every day, he will be getting the fiber that he needs every day as well. Refer to Tables 1.1 and 1.2 in Chapter 1 for proper serving sizes of foods according to your child's age. This will give you a day-by-day guide to set you up for success in the first few weeks of getting your kid on a gluten-free casein-free diet.

Look for frozen and pre-packaged foods to make your life a little less complicated. When you can not find prepared GFCF items, you may make your own by following the recipes offered in the back of this book. Shopping lists follow in the next chapter to make grocery shopping for the first two weeks a bit easier on you.

Week One

BREAKFAST

- Waffles made from scratch (recipe on p.104) (or GFCF frozen waffles) with GFCF buttery spread
- 100% pure maple syrup
- Calcium and vitamin D fortified soy milk (any time I mention or recommend soy milk, it should be calcium and vitamin D fortified, always!)
- Sliced fresh pears

SNACK

- GF pretzels
- Water

LUNCH

- Peanut butter (or any nut butter) and jelly sandwich on 2 slices GF bread (see recipe p.129)
- Cucumber slices
- Orange juice

DINNER

- Meatloaf (see recipe p.113)
- Mashed potatoes made with soy milk and GFCF buttery spread
- Cooked carrots
- Fortified soy milk

SNACK

- Rice cakes
- Fortified soy milk

DAY 2

BREAKFAST

- Fried potatoes (see recipe p.105)
- Pan fried ham
- Fried egg
- Orange juice

SNACK

- 1 cup cut-up cantaloupe melon
- 5 GFCF crackers

LUNCH

- 2 tortilla pizzas (see recipe p.112)
- Garden salad with dressing
- Fortified soy milk

DINNER

- Southwestern stuffed acorn squash (see recipe p.121)
- Brown rice
- Fortified soy milk

SNACK

- 1 cup dry GFCF breakfast cereal
- Fortified soy milk

DAY 3

BREAKFAST
- Breakfast coffee cake (see recipe p.103)
- Fortified soy milk

SNACK
- 1 orange

LUNCH
- Turkey and soy cheese sandwich on corn tortillas
- Pineapple chunks
- Fortified soy milk

DINNER
- Citrus glazed salmon (see recipe p.122)
- Brown rice
- 1 cup summer squash
- Water

SNACK
- Sugar cookies (see recipe p.173)

DAY 4

BREAKFAST
- 2 servings GF bread toasted with jam or honey
- Calcium fortified soy milk

SNACK

- Large slice of coffee cake
- Water

LUNCH

- Hotdogs and baked beans
- Orange juice

DINNER

- GFCF pizza – you can buy GF pizza shells in the freezer section of your natural food store or you can make your own crust (see recipe p.134) Make sure you use CF cheese!
- 1 cup broccoli
- Fruit juice

SNACK

- Soy yogurt

DAY 5

BREAKFAST

- GFCF breakfast cereal with calcium fortified soy milk and 1 cup strawberries

SNACK

- 2 servings GF pretzels

LUNCH

- ◦ Peanut butter and banana on a corn tortilla (see recipe p.128)
- ◦ Soy milk

DINNER

- ◦ Chicken and dumplins' (see recipe p.108)
- ◦ Steamed carrots
- ◦ Soy milk

SNACK

- ◦ Raw carrots

DAY 6

BREAKFAST

- ◦ Applesauce pancakes (see recipe p.101) with GFCF buttery spread and 100% pure maple syrup
- ◦ Calcium fortified soy milk

SNACK

- ◦ Soy yogurt with GFCF crackers

LUNCH

- ◦ Red potato and chicken salad (see recipe p.117)
- ◦ Cherry tomatoes
- ◦ Fruit juice

DINNER

- ○ Pad Thai (see recipe p.115)
- ○ Sugar snap peas – fresh or frozen
- ○ Indian quick bread (see recipe p.161)
- ○ Soy milk

SNACK

- ○ Cut-up apples with nut butter for dipping

DAY 7

BREAKFAST

- ○ Scrambled eggs and sausage
- ○ GF toast
- ○ Calcium fortified soy milk
- ○ Sliced fresh apples

SNACK

- ○ Raw carrots with GFCF dressing to dip them in
- ○ Soy milk

LUNCH

- ○ Fried rice (see recipe see p.135)
- ○ Fruit juice

DINNER

- ○ Spaghetti with tomato sauce and meatballs (see recipes pp.126 and 127)

- ○ Summer squash
- ○ GF garlic bread
- ○ Soy milk

SNACK

- ○ 1 orange

Week Two

DAY 8

BREAKFAST

- ○ Applesauce bread (see recipe p.158)
- ○ Calcium fortified soy milk

SNACK

- ○ 1 cup GF cereal
- ○ Soy milk

LUNCH

- ○ Chicken sandwich (see recipe p.151) on GF bread
- ○ GF potato chips
- ○ Orange juice

DINNER

- ○ Baked whole chicken
- ○ Baked potatoes
- ○ Steamed broccoli
- ○ Soy milk

SNACK

- Sliced cucumbers
- GF pretzels

DAY 9

BREAKFAST

- Bacon and eggs
- GFCF toast with GFCF buttery spread
- Calcium fortified soy milk
- Orange juice

SNACK

- Fresh grapes

LUNCH

- Chicken nuggets (see recipe p.130)
- French fries
- Fruit juice

DINNER

- Scallops with ginger sauce (see recipe p.118)
- Baked sweet potatoes
- Soy milk

SNACK

- 2 GF waffles with maple syrup
- Soy milk

DAY 10

BREAKFAST

- ○ Blueberry muffins (see recipe p.102)
- ○ Calcium fortified soy milk
- ○ Fresh cantaloupe melon

SNACK

- ○ Popcorn

LUNCH

- ○ Turkey chili in a can or made from scratch (see recipe p.131)
- ○ Corn bread (recipe p.157)
- ○ Soy milk

DINNER

- ○ Grilled flank steak and mixed greens salad (see recipe p.119)
- ○ Sweet rice (see recipe p.144)
- ○ Orange juice

SNACK

- ○ Cookies
- ○ Soy milk

DAY 11

BREAKFAST

- ○ GF French toast with GFCF buttery spread and 100% pure maple syrup
- ○ Fruit juice

SNACK

- ◦ Fresh cantaloupe melon

LUNCH

- ◦ Tuna sandwich (see recipe p.152) on GF bread
- ◦ Canned pears
- ◦ Soy milk

DINNER

- ◦ Hamburger patty on GF bread
- ◦ French fries
- ◦ Side salad with dressing
- ◦ Soy milk

SNACK

- ◦ Carrot sticks
- ◦ Soy milk

DAY 12

BREAKFAST

- ◦ Boiled white rice with GFCF buttery spread melted on top, a little brown sugar and some salt
- ◦ Grapes
- ◦ Fruit juice

SNACK

- ◦ Cherry tomatoes

LUNCH

- Grilled chicken breast sandwich with lettuce and tomato on GF bread
- Soy milk

DINNER

- Chili (canned or made from scratch: see recipe on p.132)
- Corn bread
- Soy milk

SNACK

- Cookies
- Soy milk

DAY 13

BREAKFAST

- Corn bread (see recipe p.157) with GFCF buttery spread
- Calcium fortified soy milk

SNACK

- Yummy peanut butter balls (see recipe p.178)
- Soy milk

LUNCH

- Ham and soy cheese sandwich on GF bread
- Carrot sticks
- Soy milk

DINNER

- Chicken curry (see recipe p.116)
- White rice
- Sliced cucumbers
- Fruit juice

SNACK

- Orange slices

DAY 14

BREAKFAST

- Instant grits
- Calcium fortified soy milk

SNACK

- Popcorn

LUNCH

- Egg sandwich (see recipe p.153) on GF bread
- Grapes
- Soy milk

DINNER

- Sweet and sour stir fry (see recipe p.133)
- White rice
- Broccoli
- Fruit juice

SNACK

- ◦ Cookies
- ◦ Soy milk

A note about cooking for the rest of the family

We have all experienced it. "What's for supper, Mum?" You reply to them – your answer doesn't suit their fancy, and whether you have taken the "If you don't like what we are having for supper, you can fix yourself a bowl of cereal" position or, much to your bewilderment, you have become a short-order cook, you know what I am talking about. How will you meet all of the family members' meal desires if one of your children is now on a restrictive diet? I have found that some meals, like tacos, for instance, satisfy everyone without having to cook something extra for the rest of the family. Spaghetti, meat sauce and garlic bread is another easy meal for the entire family. I cook rice noodles and gluten-free garlic bread for Jenny, and regular spaghetti and garlic bread for everyone else. Same with pizza: two pizzas, one with GFCF crust and CF cheese and another with regular crust and regular cheese. Now, lasagne is something that we don't eat much anymore because, first of all, it is very labor intensive in and of itself. And, second, I haven't found a great GFCF alternative. But, when we do have it, I usually serve GF spaghetti to Jenny while everyone else eats lasagne. Sometimes, everyone gets cereal for supper! This is occasionally the solution of a busy mom with needy kids, a household to run, and a husband to share it all with. I hereby proclaim to all harried moms out there: Cereal for supper is OK!

CHAPTER 10

Grocery Shopping

Grocery shopping for the GFCF diet can seem like an insurmountable task. Daunting, even. Don't fret. Take this book with you, a pencil, and your lists provided here. Go well fed, preferably alone, and get a cup of coffee – you're gonna be there for a while. Grocery shopping for the first month or so will be a new experience for you and it will take more time than it usually does. This is OK. Expect it, plan for it and go prepared – that means remembering your eyeglasses so you can see the finely printed label on the packages. Read all labels thoroughly, comparing them to the "list of ingredients to avoid" and the "list of ingredients allowed" in this book. I will consolidate and repeat the lists here in this chapter for easy reference.

Basically, meat, fruits and vegetables in their unprocessed form are gluten-free and casein-free. All bets are off once these foods are processed, however. For all other foods, reading labels is a must.

Ingredients/foods to avoid

Milk

Skim milk

Butter

Yogurt

Lactose

Powdered milk

Goat's milk

Cheese

Caseinate

Caseinates

Whey

Wheat (durum, semolina, kamut, spelt)

Rye

Barley

Triticale

Oats

Breading

Broth

Coating mixes

Communion wafers

Croutons

Imitation bacon

Imitation seafood

Marinades

Pastas

Processed meats

Roux

Sauces

Self-basting poultry

Soup bases

Stuffings

Thickeners

Brown rice syrup (frequently made from barley)

Caramel color

Dextrin (usually a corn-based product but may be derived from wheat)

Flour

Cereal products

Hydrolyzed vegetable protein (HVP)

Vegetable protein or hydrolyzed plant protein (HPP)

Textured vegetable protein (TVP)

Malt or malt flavoring (usually made from barley)

Malt vinegar

Modified food starch

Mono- and di-glycerides (in dry products only)

Flavorings in meat products

Soy sauce

Soy sauce solids

Vegetable gum

Ingredients allowed

Rice	Arrowroot
Corn	Amaranth
Potato	Tef
Tapioca	Nut flours
Beans	Soy
Sorghum	Fruit – pure
Quinoa	Fruit juice – pure
Millet	Vegetables
Buckwheat	Meat – unprocessed

You need to read every ingredient on the food label and compare it to this list. The minute you see one of the forbidden ingredients, put the food item back on the shelf. After about a month, you will know what you can stock in your pantry and what you can not. It just gets easier from this point on. Remember to always read labels before buying even a familiar and previously acceptable product because recipes change, and manufacturers change. Reading ingredient labels is the most important task to ensure that your child will remain on a GFCF diet.

The lists that follow will stock your pantry, fridge and freezer for the next two weeks and beyond. Build your grocery shopping list from the following.

Staples to always have on hand

Pantry

- ○ Red wine vinegar
- ○ Mirin (sweet rice wine)
- ○ Fish sauce (found in Asian section of grocery store)

- Lemon juice
- Rice milk
- Infant rice cereal
- Plain popcorn
- Raisins
- GFCF chicken bouillon granules
- Applesauce
- 100% maple syrup
- Non-stick cooking spray
- Peanut butter
- Other nut butters (sunflower butter ROCKS!)
- Jelly or jams
- Orange marmalade
- Brown rice
- White rice
- Hot red pepper sauce
- Honey
- Walnuts
- Dijon style mustard

Canned foods

- Canned coconut milk
- Canned pears
- Canned tuna fish
- Canned pineapple chunks

Oils

- Canola oil
- Olive oil
- Sesame oil
- Peanut oil

Spices

- Pumpkin pie spice
- Cayenne pepper
- Cinnamon
- Dried parsley
- Onion powder
- Garlic powder
- Chili powder
- Cumin
- Crushed red pepper
- Curry powder
- Ground black pepper or black pepper for grinding

Baking supplies

- White rice flour
- Brown rice flour
- Potato starch flour
- Tapioca starch flour
- Soy flour
- Buckwheat flour
- Corn starch
- Xanthan gum (located next to the alternative flours)
- GF mixture I or II – already made up and stored in an airtight container
- Fine yellow corn meal
- Sugar
- Brown sugar
- Confectioners' sugar
- Baking soda
- Baking powder
- Salt
- Shortening

Refrigerated

- ○ GFCF buttery spread
- ○ Fresh minced garlic
- ○ Jar of prepared horseradish
- ○ Salad dressing
- ○ Real mayonnaise

Frozen

- ○ GFCF waffles
- ○ Frozen carrots
- ○ Frozen broccoli
- ○ Frozen sugar snap peas
- ○ Frozen peas and carrots
- ○ Frozen blueberries
- ○ Frozen french fries
- ○ GF bread for the freezer

Week one shopping list

All staples listed above plus:

Fresh veggies

- ○ Summer squash
- ○ Cherry tomatoes
- ○ Green onions
- ○ Potatoes
- ○ Red potatoes
- ○ Carrots
- ○ Onions
- ○ Veggies for salad
- ○ Acorn squash
- ○ Red bell pepper

- ◦ Cucumbers
- ◦ Fresh ginger
- ◦ Fresh dill

Fresh fruits

- ◦ Pears
- ◦ Apples
- ◦ Oranges
- ◦ Bananas
- ◦ Strawberries
- ◦ Cantaloupe melon

Dairy alternatives

- ◦ Soy yogurt – make sure it is calcium fortified, with 30 percent of the daily value coming from 1 serving or 8 oz (225g).
- ◦ Soy milk – make sure it is calcium and vitamin D fortified labeled as 30 percent of the daily value for calcium and vitamin D coming from 1 serving or 8 oz (225g).
- ◦ GFCF non-dairy cheese – slices and shredded for pizza.

Proteins

- ◦ Eggs
- ◦ 2 lb salmon (fresh or frozen)
- ◦ Hotdogs
- ◦ 1 whole chicken
- ◦ Boneless skinless chicken breasts
- ◦ GFCF sausage
- ◦ GFCF turkey sausage
- ◦ Lean ground beef
- ◦ GF deli ham
- ◦ GF deli turkey

Pantry

- Dry white wine
- Baked beans
- Sliced almonds
- Small jar of pimentos
- Black olives
- GF soy sauce
- GFCF breakfast cereal
- GF bread
- GF pretzels
- GFCF rice cakes
- GFCF crackers
- 6 inch corn tortillas
- GFCF tomato sauce
- Canned stewed tomatoes
- Black beans

Refrigerated

- Orange juice

Frozen

- GFCF frozen pizza shell

Week two shopping list

Make sure you still have all of your staple items and:

Fresh veggies

- Broccoli
- Cucumbers

- Sweet potatoes
- Green onions
- Baby carrots
- Lettuce
- Tomato
- Cherry tomatoes
- Green pepper
- Red pepper
- Veggies for garden salad

Fresh Fruits

- Apples
- Oranges
- Grapes
- Cantaloupe melon

Dairy alternatives

- Soy milk – rules stated previously still apply
- CF soy cheese

Proteins

- Eggs
- 1 whole chicken
- Boneless chicken breasts
- Bacon
- Medium sea scallops
- Flank steak
- Hamburger patties or fresh ground hamburger
- GFCF deli ham

Pantry

- GF bread
- GF pretzels
- GFCF cookies
- GFCF potato chips
- GFCF puffed rice cereal
- GFCF instant grits cereal
- Canned GFCF chili
- Canned GFCF turkey chili

Refrigerated

- Orange juice

Usually, I will go to three different grocery stores every two weeks to get all of the items that I need. This is because one store doesn't carry Jenny's favorite soy pudding. Another doesn't carry her favorite flavor in soy yogurt. And yet another has the cereal bar that she loves. I have found that if you frequent a grocery store and spend a lot of time (and money!) there, quite often it will be advantageous for you to introduce yourself to the manager. Many times, when a store does not carry an item that I need, I will request that the manager order it special for me. He is then assured of my repeat business. For example, I shop at a grocery store in Petersburg, Virginia, that carries brown rice flour, but does not carry white rice flour. The same chain in the neighboring town sold the white rice flour. I asked the manager of the Petersburg store if he could carry white rice flour, on a regular basis, for me. The next week, when I went in, there it was! If you can get your favorite store to carry all the items that you need, this will reduce the number of stores you will need to visit each week, thus saving time, money, and gasoline!

CHAPTER 11

But My Child is Such a Fussy Eater!

When chatting with other moms of autistic children I wondered why on earth they would not at least try the GFCF diet as an intervention strategy for their child. I heard things like:

"My child is such a fussy eater!"

"I just think it would be too difficult to do."

"I don't have time to cook or bake from scratch."

"When I checked with his doctor, he said that he'd seen more kids harmed by poor nutrition from the diet than helped by the diet."

"He loves milk – I don't think he could live without it."

or the classic:

"All he will eat is pizza, macaroni and cheese, and cheese-flavored crackers, I can't take these foods away from him. What would he eat?"

All of these concerns are reality for each of these moms. Autistic spectrum kids are usually picky eaters with sensory issues around food anyway, and then, on top of that, try and introduce a brand new way of eating (translate: change in routine) – what a recipe for disaster! In this chapter, I hope to give you some strategies to get around all of these concerns.

Lots of times, we can find alternatives that come close to the highly coveted foods. Sometimes, we just need to be patient through the first three weeks (which can seem like an eternity when you are in it). I know from our experience, when Jenny discovered how good she felt after eating the GFCF way for about a week, she didn't crave or want the other stuff! She realized how sick she felt when she was eating gluten and casein. Jenny is not the only child that has expressed this realization. I have heard the same thing from other moms as well.

First and foremost, if a child is hungry, he is going to eat. Don't be afraid to let him get hungry. He is not going to die.

Second, establish a routine of meals and snacks at regular intervals so that the child can expect and anticipate his next meal.

Then, don't let him fill up on high calorie liquids (like juice or soda) or on empty calorie snacks (like chips or cookies) in between meals. Allow only water in between set meals and snacks so that hunger can set in. This will assure better compliance at the table when it is time to sit down and eat. This will set the stage for compliance of the GFCF diet. Keep this schedule rather rigid during the first three weeks; children need and want structure, especially during a big time of change, which is what this is for them. Being able to predict meal time and snack time will give them a sense of being in control, which will offer comfort during what can be perceived as a difficult time.

Remember to put very small amounts of food on the plate. Overwhelming a child with large portion sizes always adds up to disaster. Allow the child to ask for more food or more drink. This gives him power and control when he may feel powerless and out of control. Consider serving dessert with the meal to avoid the "you have to finish your meal before you can have dessert" struggle or to de-emphasize dessert as being more valuable than the vegetables on the plate.

Make meals and snacks fun. Name the new-to-them foods. Like, "Mom's Monster Truck Meatloaf" and allow everyone to bring a truck to the table when you serve this meatloaf, or "Daddy's Do-a-Dance Stew" and before you sit down and eat, everyone has to do a silly dance. Have your child come up with names for foods based on what the food looks like. Watch out, some might be extra-disgusting, like Greasy Hair Spaghetti and Eyeball Meatballs.

Maybe your child has a favorite super hero or television character. Name the supper, casserole or sandwich after the super hero or favorite character. Have theme meals like Taco Tuesday, and watch a movie during supper on TV trays every Tuesday night of each week. Friday may be Pizza night, and every Friday, you serve pizza. Again, drawing in the predictability factor always equals a win for your child whose world might be turned upside down by the change in diet.

Make sure that mealtime conversation is positive and light-hearted. Talk about all the good things your child did that day and praise him for good behavior at the supper table. Never discuss upsetting topics or bad news over dinner.

Cutting foods into interesting shapes can entice picky eaters to be interested in their food. Have a Triangle lunch – and cut everything into triangles, including the napkins! Use fun cookie cutters to get sandwiches or luncheon meats into different shapes. Give your child a choice of what shape he would like his food cut into; you may even let him cut it with a cookie cutter (under your supervision, of course). Make faces on the plate with the foods: two triangle sandwich pieces for eyes, a grape for the nose, and carrot sticks lined up as a mouth may interest him in eating.

Have the child prepare the meal with you or by himself (with you as an observer or coach). Lots of times, kids will be much more interested in eating something that they have prepared. Be careful that one food doesn't touch another food. Have special plates, bowls and utensils for your child, or serve the new foods on old familiar favorite plates and bowls, using familiar utensils.

You, as the invested parent, may have to eat the GFCF way for a while. Remember that our kids learn from our actions, and not from our words. If you won't eat it, why should they? Be a role model – the picky eater stops here. If you as the parent are a picky eater, what else do you expect from your child?

Finding alternatives to the once-craved, highly coveted foods takes some time and patience. Identify GFCF foods that your child really enjoys and whenever he asks for the "old" cheese-flavored crackers or the macaroni and cheese that he used to eat by the box-full, have some alternative GFCF foods on hand that will take his attention away from the gluten, casein laden foods. Jenny loves soy ice cream and that is a real treat for her. She also loves the soy pudding. She can eat GF pasta until it comes out of her ears. I really thought that finding alternatives would be difficult, but it has not been; she has taken to the GFCF alternatives very well.

Finally, never force your child to eat. If he eats just a very small amount of food for supper, accept this, offer him his bedtime snack at the routine time, and tomorrow will be another day. If you hold to your schedule, you are calm about the amounts that he is choosing to eat, and not offering snacks or caloric liquids in between routine meal times and snack times, your picky eater will learn that he better eat what is served to him while he has the chance. You must not make this a control issue. Your responsibility is to serve healthy meals at regular times; his responsibility is to choose to eat it or not, and to choose how much he will eat. Keep your responsibility separate from his responsibility. You have no business asking or demanding that he eats more or that he eats this or that or that he eats at all. After three weeks of this, he will start feeling better physically and mentally, he will stop craving the usual macaroni and cheese and cheese-flavored crackers, and he will accept the GFCF foods without incident.

CHAPTER 12

Dealing with Special Occasions Involving Food

It never fails. You start your kid up on the Gluten-Free Casein-Free Diet, all is going well and then BAM! You get invited to a social function. Now what? First and foremost, don't panic! Here are ways that we have dealt with just a few situations that can cause trouble without some careful thought or without planning ahead. A small travel cooler and a couple of little ice packs will take you far on the special occasion road. You may also want to purchase multiple sizes of take-along containers to assure that you have what you need when the time comes.

For events that you will be attending with your child, you have control over what is brought, and what is eaten, for the most part. The tricky part is when the event is at school or at day care, and you will not be there. It also gets tricky if you don't know about the event ahead of time, and no GFCF food is sent in or available to accommodate your child. There are a few ways to get around this. I have always informed the teachers/aides/day-care providers of Jenny's diet and asked them not to allow her to have anything that isn't sent in from home. They will typically allow me to stock their pantry, refrigerator and freezer at their site, so that she always has a GFCF option, even in times when a treat or party is not planned in advance or I am not notified ahead of time. I provide the school and day care with a huge airtight tin full of GFCF snacks that I restock regularly, I often provide soy yogurt, pudding, soy milk and other desserts and goodies for the fridge, and I also provide soy ice cream for their freezer. Having the GFCF diet written into the Individualized Education Plan (IEP) at school is always a good idea as it motivates staff to keep these special snacks on hand for her, and to serve them to her instead of the food that may come in for parties and special occasions.

The pancake breakfast

The key to staying true to the diet during any special occasion is to know ahead of time, and to plan for it. For pancake breakfasts, and pancake suppers for that matter, I cook up a batch of GFCF pancakes, and bring a stack along with us. I also pack Jenny's GFCF buttery spread and her GFCF syrup as well. You can never tell what will be served and you don't ever want to assume that what they will be serving will be GFCF. Most butters and margarines have casein in them, and some syrups do as well.

The spaghetti supper

For the spaghetti supper, again, I make up a batch of GF spaghetti, sauce and garlic bread, pack it in the cooler, and when we arrive and find our seats, I plate the food, and ask that it be heated up. Jenny can then enjoy the same meal that everyone else is eating. The only person that knows she is eating anything different is the microwave attendant and maybe a few people sitting at our table. It is easy to be discreet about these things, if you wish. The only give away is that you walk in with a large paper bag or travel-size cooler.

The pot luck or covered dish

The pot luck supper is tricky in that you don't know what is in the dishes that everyone else has brought, but you can easily bring something that is GFCF for your child to eat. Don't take a chance with the other dishes; just let your child know that what you have brought is what he or she will eat. I will usually bring a main dish and dessert, so Jenny will be assured of those two meal items. Lots of times, when I bring GFCF brownies, no one can tell that they are GFCF!

The pizza party

The key to the pizza party is, again, to know about it ahead of time, so that you can send in some GFCF pizza with your child to be heated up when the party starts. Pizza travels well in tin foil, packed in a lunch-size cooler, with little ice packs. I have also sent it in on a plate wrapped in tin foil, but it doesn't travel as well that way.

The ice cream social

The ice cream social works well when you have the ice cream already stocked in the facility freezer. Lots of toppings are GFCF, and you can provide them as well, or ask the staff for a list of what will be served and inform them in writing which toppings your child is allowed to eat. Lots of times after the child has been on the diet for a while, they can tell the staff what is acceptable and what is not.

A bag lunch

The bag lunch becomes routine easy after a while, but when you are just starting out, it may seem overwhelming. Start with a portable juice, some carrot sticks, a GFCF sandwich, like peanut butter and jelly on GF bread, some GFCF potato chips and some GFCF cookies. No sweat.

Travelling

Travelling is tough. Again, the key is to have enough GFCF food on the trip with you. Pack bags and a cooler full of special food for your child; keep it in the car, not in the trunk. Before you get to your destination, research grocery stores in the area that will have a natural foods section where you can get his or her favorite GFCF snacks and foods. Call family and friends that you may be visiting ahead of time, and ask them specifically to have the GFCF foods on hand before you arrive. My mother-in-law always bakes special treats for Jenny before we visit, and freezes them, so that when Jenny arrives to their lake house, she has breakfast breads, and desserts to enjoy, just like everyone else. Lots of resorts and vacation spots are keen on the GFCF diet and the chefs have had special training on the diet because it is becoming so widespread. You may want to call the place that you will be staying at in advance and ask if their chefs have had special training on cooking for the GFCF diet. When we went to Disney World, we had the easiest time, because all of the chefs as well as the wait staff were trained on the diet. Sometimes, the chef would actually come out to the table and take her order. If the wait staff and chefs have not been trained, do not be afraid or shy to order special requests for your child. For instance, if you order a baked potato, ask that it be dry – no butter, no sour cream. Ask that salad not be dressed, and bring your own salad dressing or use oil and vinegar as dressing. When we eat out, I will order plain meat or chicken, grilled and a large side of vegetables, steamed with no butter for Jenny. Be clear when you order that your child is on a special diet for health reasons. You don't need to say anything else. Using the "allergy" word is also a good strategy, because that will get the staff's attention, and they will be extra careful in the preparation of your child's food.

The school party

This is when you pull out all your resources, and resort to the snacks in the airtight tin, the stocked refrigerator, and the freezer. Try to find out what will be served at the party and provide something similar. For instance, if it is a cupcake and juice party, provide GFCF cupcakes for your child. Always send in something that your child can eat, or else you will have to resort to what is there, and I can guarantee you, it will not be GFCF!

When we first started this diet, we got a lot of questions from family, friends, and teachers. I heard overtones of doubt and often the unsaid was "Why would you go to all that trouble?" It is best to ignore the negative and to believe in what you are doing because you know what is best for your child. Asking for support was my first line of defense; it can be yours, too. I also wrote her GFCF diet into her IEP, so that the school had to abide by the diet according to the law. Over the years, I have found a fine balance between telling people about her special diet and being discreet about it. And in the end, if you are met with opposition or are not supported, then you change the circumstances so they meet your needs. Do not be hesitant to change child-care arrangements to something more suitable. Do not stay with people that are unsupportive of your efforts in giving your child the best life that he or she can have.

CHAPTER 13

Other Stuff to Consider

You want my advice? Don't read this chapter until you have your kid up and running with the Gluten-Free Casein-Free Diet for at lease three months. It takes about three months to see all of the benefits of the diet. Then, you really need to be at this baseline for a while to know what is "normal" (I know, strange use of the word, right?) behavior and what is not. Then you will be able to see which GFCF foods cause a "reaction" and what a "reaction" actually is, for your child. This is a very individualized phenomenon.

For Jenny, after three weeks of casein-free, we introduced gluten-free. I was so overwhelmed by the whole process, I couldn't even consider removing other specific foods, dyes, preservatives or artificial sweeteners at the beginning. But as time passed and we saw improvement in speech patterns and behavior, I could notice a regression every time she ate chocolate, bananas, and strawberries, or anything strawberry flavored. She would revert back to her inappropriate touching, repeating the same phrases over and over and obsessing over things for hours. Basically, you want to pay specific attention to how your child behaves and what he had to eat. If you can start to see a pattern like I did with Jenny and strawberries, you know that you will probably want to avoid that food or products with that food in it.

Some other common offenders besides gluten and casein are corn and soy, artificial food colorings, especially Yellow #5 or

Tartrazine and Red #40, and common preservatives like BHA, BHT and TBHQ. I know at this point that all of this looks like a foreign language to you. I will break it down in understandable English throughout this chapter. I will also recommend a book by Doris Rapp called *Is This Your Child?*. Doris does a wonderful job in her book describing behavior changes as a result of food allergies, food intolerances and food sensitivities.

Your child may be sensitive or intolerant to corn and products made from corn. Try eliminating these foods from his or her diet for three days and see what happens. If behavior improves, you know that these foods should be avoided as well. If you see no difference in behavior, you may re-introduce the corn. Along with corn, soy is commonly a problem food. You will only want to eliminate one food at a time, so after you try the elimination of corn, wait about a week and then try the elimination of soy and soy products. Observe for changes; if you see an improvement after you remove the soy, you may want to eliminate the soy from the diet.

Artificial colorings, especially Yellow #5 or Tartrazine and Red #40, have also been identified as offenders (Rowe *et al*, 1994; Weiss *et al.* 1980). Look for these ingredients when reading the food label. You may simply want to avoid all food colorings for a period of a week and see if behavior improves. In order to do this, you will have to read labels diligently, shop for unprocessed food and make almost everything from scratch. Personally, I feel much better when I eat food without artificial coloring or preservatives. I have less muscle aches and more energy. Both my kids do better on this type of diet as well.

BHA, BHT and TBHQ are substances added to food *and cosmetics* to prevent the spoilage of fat, thus preserving the product and enabling it to sit on the shelf for a longer period of time. A "longer shelf life" is attractive to the food and cosmetic industry trying to sell the product. The problem is that although the research is inconclusive at this time, some studies suggest that these additives may cause cancer (US Department of Health and Human Services 2005).

From personal experience, I can attest to the fact that when Jenny follows a gluten-free casein-free diet that is also free of additives and preservatives, she is happier, more "with it" and has very little (almost no) undesirable behavior.

Dr. Ben F. Feingold, MD was a pediatrician and an allergist who pioneered a controversial diet in the 1970s to treat hyperactivity in children (Feingold 1975). The Feingold Diet, as it is called today, eliminates artificial colorings, artificial flavorings, aspartame, three petroleum-based preservatives, and, initially, some salicylates. Some doctors believe that the diet does not have any affect on behavior, while others, along with people living with Attention Deficit Hyperactivity Disorder (ADHD), and parents of ADHD kids, use the diet in place of their ADHD medication (Reichenberg-Ullman and Ullman 1996).

CHAPTER 14

Gluten-Free
Casein-Free Power Foods

10 GFCF power foods

In this chapter, ten power foods will be identified. These gluten-free casein-free nutritional stars contain antioxidants, vitamins and minerals that will benefit your family's health in many ways. I will also help you to find ways to include these nutritional power packs into your diet creatively and easily. Your daughter won't touch spinach? Don't worry – we will disguise it! It will transform itself into spaghetti sauce! Use this chapter as a reference when you have run out of ideas, or you have exhausted the menus provided in Chapter 9. Some of the nutrition information is repeated here as you might skip over a section that doesn't interest you, like the section on walnuts if someone in your family has a nut allergy. The information from Pennington and Douglas (2004), is included over and over as it applies to each food category.

Antioxidants are a group of compounds that occur naturally in foods. They protect us from damage caused by free radicals which can injure healthy cells and are thought to play a role in cancer, heart disease, arthritis, cataract formation, memory loss and aging. Antioxidants include vitamins E and C, carotenoids such as beta-carotene and lycopene, polyphenols and flavonoids.

Phytochemicals are chemicals that are found in plants that contain protective, disease-preventing compounds. It is estimated that there may be more than 100 different phytochemicals in just one serving of vegetables – a complex combination impossible to put in pill form. Phytochemicals appear to help your body fight off cancer-causing agents, and enhance the body's immune function. Broccoli and leafy green vegetables are examples of foods rich in phytochemicals and, usually, the darker the color of the fruit or vegetable, the more phytochemicals it contains.

Nuts / seeds

Walnuts are great sources of omega-3 fatty acids, which improve cholesterol levels and prevent heart disease. Nuts are high in fiber which helps the bowels to stay regular. Nuts are also high in unsaturated fat which, when eaten in moderation, can help reduce the "bad" cholesterol and raise the "good" cholesterol. Nuts are a great source of energy for growing kids.

Almonds, cashews, peanuts and walnuts are high in a vitamin called biotin which helps in the formation of fatty acids, works in the metabolism of amino acids and carbohydrates, and is necessary for normal growth and development and promotes overall good health. Peanuts are high in choline, a vitamin that maintains cell membrane integrity, and works in the function of the nervous system, which includes regulating mood, behavior, orientation, personality traits and judgment. Almonds, brazil nuts, hazelnuts, peanuts, sunflower seeds and walnuts are high in vitamin E which promotes normal growth and development, promotes normal red blood cell formation and improves immunity. Peanuts are also high in niacin, which aids in the release of energy from foods, and also helps to synthesize DNA. Peanuts and sunflower seeds are high in pantothenic acid, which is necessary in the process of energy metabolism of carbohydrates, protein and fat. Hazelnuts and sunflower seeds are high in pyridoxine necessary for protein, carbohydrate and fat utilization. Peanuts are high in thiamine which promotes normal growth and development, and is necessary for converting carbohydrates into energy in muscles and in the nervous system. Almonds and brazil nuts are high in calcium, which is necessary for normal activity of the nervous, muscular and skeletal systems, builds bones and teeth, maintains bone density and strength, helps regulate heartbeat, blood clotting, muscle contraction, promotes normal growth and development and promotes storage and release of some body hormones. Nuts are high in copper, which promotes normal red blood cell formation, assists in production of several enzymes involved in respiration, and promotes normal insulin function. Nuts are also high in magnesium which activates essential enzymes, affects metabolism of protein, helps to transport sodium and potassium across cell membranes, influences calcium levels inside cells and aids in muscle contractions. Hazelnuts and pecans are high in manganese, which promotes normal growth and development, promotes nerve function and helps promote blood clotting. Almonds, peanuts and sunflower seeds are high in phosporus, which helps in the utilization of B-complex vitamins, works with calcium to build strong bones and teeth, promotes energy metabolism, promotes growth, and aids in the maintenance and repair of all body tissues in the healing process. Nuts are high in potassium, which promotes regular heartbeat, normal muscle contraction, maintains water balance in the body, and maintains normal function of brain, skeletal muscles and kidneys. Sesame seeds and sunflower seeds are high in the mineral zinc, which promotes normal growth and development, aids in wound healing, maintains normal taste and sense of smell and helps in the process of moving carbon dioxide out of the tissues to the lungs.

Spinach

Spinach is high in vitamin A which helps in the prevention of night blindness, promotes bone growth, teeth development, helps form and maintain healthy skin, hair, mucous membranes and builds the body's resistance to infection. Spinach is also high in vitamin C which aids in iron absorption, helps heal wounds, prevents scurvy, promotes healthy capillaries, gums and teeth, helps form collagen in connective tissue, increases calcium absorption and reduces free radical production. Spinach is high in vitamin E, which promotes normal growth and development and promotes normal red blood cell formation. Vitamin E acts as an antioxidant in the body and thus improves immune function. Spinach also provides vitamin K which is necessary for normal blood clotting. Spinach is high in copper which promotes normal red blood cell formation, assists in production of several enzymes involved in respiration and promotes normal insulin function. And spinach is also high in potassium which promotes regular heartbeat, normal muscle contraction, maintains water balance in body and maintains normal function of the brain, skeletal muscles and kidneys. Spinach ranges in taste from mild to bitter. It can be used raw (as in the spinach salad recipe featured on p.147), cooked, steamed or sauteed.

Green leafies

Expect delicious flavor and variety in your salad or meal from green leafy vegetables. In addition to fiber, green leafy vegetables also provide lots of vitamins and minerals. Kale has a similar taste to cabbage, but is milder. Try it sauteed in a bit of olive oil with garlic. Collards taste similar to kale and cabbage. Collards make a wonderful side dish. Green leafy vegetables are high in vitamin A, which helps in the prevention of night blindness, promotes bone growth, teeth development, helps form and maintain healthy skin, hair, mucous membranes and builds the body's resistance to infection. Green leafy vegetables are also high in vitamin C which aids iron absorption, helps heal wounds, prevents scurvy, promotes healthy capillaries, gums and teeth, helps form collagen in connective tissue, increases calcium absorption, and reduces free radical production.

Green leafies are high in folic acid, which is important for normal red blood cell formation, necessary for normal patterns of growth and development. Folic acid also helps in the metabolism of amino acids and protein synthesis, and helps prevent birth defects. Collard greens are high in pantothenic acid which is necessary in the process of energy metabolism of carbohydrates, protein and fat. Green leafy vegetables provide vitamin K necessary for normal blood clotting. Green leafy vegetables are high in magnesium, which activates essential enzymes, affects metabolism of protein, helps to transport sodium and potassium across cell membranes, influences calcium levels inside cells and aids in muscle contraction. Green leafy vegetables are high in a mineral called molybdenum, which promotes normal growth and development and aids in the elimination of waste in the urine. Cabbage is high in selenium, which works as an antioxidant and promotes normal growth and development.

Soy

Soy is a great source of protein. It can easily be substituted for meat in the diet. Soybeans are high in biotin, which helps in the formation of fatty acids, works in the metabolism of amino acids and carbohydrates, is necessary for normal growth and development and promotes good overall health. Soybeans are also high in choline, which maintains cell membrane integrity and works in the function of the nervous system, which regulates mood, behavior, orientation, personality traits and judgement. Soybeans are high in niacin, a B vitamin that aids in the release of energy from foods and helps to synthesize DNA. Soybeans are also high in pantothenic acid, which is necessary in the process of energy metabolism of carbohydrates, protein and fat. Soybeans are high in pyridoxine, which is necessary for protein, carbohydrate and fat utilization. Tofu, a curd made from soybeans, is high in calcium. Calcium is necessary for normal activity of the nervous, muscular and skeletal systems, builds bones and teeth, maintains bone density and strength, helps to regulate heartbeat, blood clotting, muscle contraction, promotes normal growth and development, and promotes the storage and release of some body hormones. Soybeans are high in copper, which promotes normal red blood cell formation, assists in the production of several enzymes involved in respiration, and promotes normal insulin function. Soybeans are also high in phosphorus which helps in the utilization of B-complex vitamins, works with calcium to build strong bones and teeth, promotes energy metabolism, and promotes growth, maintenance and repair of all body tissues in the healing process. Soybeans are high in zinc, a mineral that promotes normal growth and development, aids wound healing, maintains normal taste and sense of smell, and helps in the process of moving carbon dioxide out of tissues to the lungs.

Broccoli

Broccoli is one of the cruciferous vegetables loaded with antioxidants. Broccoli is high in vitamin A which helps in the prevention of night blindness, promotes bone growth, teeth development, helps form and maintain healthy skin, hair, mucous membranes, and builds the body's resistance to infection. Broccoli is also high in vitamin C which aids iron absorption, helps heal wounds, prevents scurvy, promotes healthy capillaries, gums and teeth, helps form collagen in connective tissue, increases calcium absorption and reduces free radical production. (One cup of broccoli has more vitamin C than an orange!) Broccoli is high in vitamin E, which promotes normal growth and development, promotes normal red blood cell formation, is an antioxidant and improves immunity. Broccoli is high in pantothenic acid, which is necessary in the process of energy metabolism of carbohydrates, protein and fats. Broccoli is high in vitamin K, which is necessary for normal blood clotting. Broccoli is high in calcium which is necessary for normal activity of the nervous, muscular and skeletal systems, builds bones and teeth, maintains bone density and strength, helps to regulate heartbeat, blood clotting, muscle contraction, promotes normal growth and development, and promotes the storage and release of some body hormones. And, finally, broccoli is high in selenium, which works as an antioxidant and promotes normal growth and development.

Avocados

Avocados are high in vitamin E, an antioxidant that promotes normal growth and development and normal red blood cell formation. Vitamin E also improves immunity. Avocados are high in folic acid which aids in normal red blood cell formation, is necessary for normal patterns of growth and development, and helps in metabolism of amino acids and protein synthesis. Avocados are high in pantothenic acid, which is necessary in the process of energy metabolism of carbohydrates, protein and fat. Avocados are high in pyridoxine, which is necessary for protein, carbohydrate and fat utilization. Avocados are high in copper, which promotes normal red blood cell formation, assists in the production of several enzymes involved in respiration, and promotes normal insulin function. Avocados are high in magnesium, which activates essential enzymes, affects metabolism of protein, helps to transport sodium and potassium across the cell membrane, influences calcium levels inside cells and aids in muscle contraction. Avocados are also high in potassium, which promotes a regular heartbeat, promotes normal muscle contraction, maintains water balance in the body and maintains the normal function of the brain, skeletal muscles and kidneys.

Bananas

Bananas are high in biotin, which helps with the formation of fatty acids, works in the metabolism of amino acids and carbohydrates, and is necessary for normal growth, development and good health.

Bananas are high in folic acid, which is essential for normal red blood cell formation, necessary for normal patterns of growth and development and helps in the metabolism of amino acids and in protein synthesis. Bananas are high in pantothenic acid, which is necessary in the process of energy metabolism of carbohydrates, protein and fat. Bananas are high in pyridoxine, which is necessary for protein, carbohydrate and fat utilization. Bananas are a good source of riboflavin, which is needed for normal tissue respiration, and works in conjunction with other B vitamins to promote normal growth and development. Bananas are high in magnesium, which activates essential enzymes, affects metabolism of protein, helps to transport sodium and potassium across the cell membrane, influences calcium levels inside cells and aids in muscle contraction. And, as most people know, bananas are high in potassium, which promotes regular heartbeat, promotes normal muscle contraction, maintains water balance in the body and maintains the normal function of the brain, skeletal muscles and kidneys.

Oranges

Oranges are high in vitamin C, which aids iron absorption, helps heal wounds, prevents scurvy, promotes healthy capillaries, gums and teeth, helps form collagen in connective tissue, increases calcium absorption and reduces free radical production. Oranges are high in folic acid, which is essential for normal red blood cell formation, necessary for normal patterns of growth and development and helps in the metabolism of amino acids and in protein synthesis. Oranges are high in pantothenic acid, which is necessary in the process of energy metabolism of carbohydrates, protein and fat. Oranges are high in thiamine, which is necessary to promote normal growth and development and necessary for converting carbohydrates into energy in muscles and in the nervous system. And oranges are high in potassium, which promotes regular heartbeat, promotes normal muscle contraction, maintains water balance in the body and maintains the normal function of the brain, skeletal muscles and kidneys.

Potatoes

Potatoes are high in vitamin C which aids iron absorption, helps heal wounds, prevents scurvy, promotes healthy capillaries, gums and teeth, helps form collagen in connective tissue, increases calcium absorption and reduces free radical production. Potatoes are high in niacin, which aids in the release of energy from foods and helps to synthesize DNA. Potatoes are high in pyridoxine, which is necessary for protein, carbohydrate and fat utilization. And potatoes are high in potassium, which promotes regular heartbeat, promotes normal muscle contraction, maintains water balance in the body and maintains the normal function of the brain, skeletal muscles and kidneys.

Asparagus

Asparagus are high in vitamin A which helps in the prevention of night blindness, promotes bone growth, teeth development, helps form and maintain healthy skin, hair and mucous membranes, and builds the body's resistance to infection. Asparagus is also a good source of vitamin E, an antioxidant that promotes normal growth and development and normal red blood cell formation. Vitamin E also improves immunity. Asparagus provides high levels of folic acid which is essential for normal red blood cell formation, necessary for normal patterns of growth and development and helps in the metabolism of amino acids and in protein synthesis. And asparagus provides vitamin K, which is necessary for normal blood clotting. Finally, asparagus is high in potassium which promotes regular heartbeat, promotes normal muscle contraction, maintains water balance in the body and maintains the normal function of the brain, skeletal muscles and kidneys.

To keep the "power" in the "power foods," remember that fresh is better, as cooking can destroy some important phytochemicals. Frozen fruits and vegetables are nearly as good as fresh and may even be more nutritious than fresh fruits and vegetables that have been stored for weeks or months in transport under conditions that prevent proper ripening. Canned fruits and vegetables are usually fine, though many come loaded with lots of salt and sugar. Don't overcook or use lots of water when cooking. Steaming and blanching are best.

How can we fit spinach into the diet of a child that won't eat anything green? Mostly, we disguise it! We sneak it in where they would least expect it. My favorite trick is to add a whole block of frozen spinach into my meat sauce and serve it over spaghetti. The spinach gives the sauce a delicious flavor and adds lots of body. It thickens the sauce up and my family loves it! We also use fresh spinach leaves as if they were lettuce. We add them to sandwiches, wraps and salads. You can also serve noodles over a bed of sauteed spinach. We add spinach to eggs at breakfast. There are lots of ways to "hide" the good stuff in with well-accepted foods; you just need to think out of the box and get a bit creative!

CHAPTER 15

The Journey

I have learned some lessons over the years! In the past, if I couldn't do it "right" (that is, perfect) then I wouldn't do it at all. I was proud to be a perfectionist. I boasted that quality in all of my job interviews. Then, I grew up and served cereal to my family, for supper.

When Jenny was born, I was convinced I would be the perfect mother. I would do everything right, make no mistakes. I had my "What to Expect in the First Year" manual – what else would I need? As you know, those manuals don't apply to our special kids. I had to put that manual away, and trust myself, something that I had never done before. Uncharted water. I was fortunate enough to stumble across Karyn Seroussi's book, *Unraveling the Mystery of Autism and Pervasive Developmental Disorder* (2002), and decided to try the GFCF diet with Jenny. Maybe it would make a difference. So, with an open mind I set out on a journey – what I thought would be a mere science experiment turned into the greatest discovery of my life, so far. Yes, Jenny did improve, and we saw the improvements as quickly as three weeks, more to come at three months and then on and on, the progress continued. But most importantly I have learned lessons more valuable, more universal than better speech patterns and less perseverating. I have learned patience, acceptance, and tolerance. It is with strength and persistence that I parent my children, but also myself, with these new found qualities. I accept less than perfect from my kids, striving everyday to be the best mom

I can be. But, more importantly, I accept less than perfect from myself, striving to be the best "me" I can be.

Today, Jenny is 14 and Christine is 10. They are both healthy, vibrant young ladies, thriving in a world that is moving too fast.

With Christine's arrival into my life, I finally got to visit Italy. To me, Italy is over-rated, but I am sure glad I got a taste of the fruit there. We hang out in Holland, mostly. It is a place that I had tried to get out of so desperately as a child and young adult, but I have become very comfortable there, and actually prefer it now... Holland has become my home.

PART III

The Cookbook

Before you jump in and start cooking and baking up a gluten-free casein-free storm, you may want to equip your kitchen like anyone would equip their garage with the right tools. I have found that to do this thing right, you will need a food processor, a bread machine, a stand-up mixer with a pasta machine attachment, or a separate pasta-making machine, a slow cooker, and a waffle iron. These tools will simplify your task ahead.

CHAPTER 16

Alternative Flour Mixtures

GF flour mixture 1

Ingredients

2 cups white rice flour

1/3 cup tapioca starch flour

2/3 cup potato starch flour

3 tsp xanthan gum

For each cup of wheat flour, substitute this mixture, cup for cup.

GF flour mixture 2

Ingredients

2½ cups rice flour

1 cup tapioca flour

¼ cup bean flour

1 cup potato starch flour

¼ cup cornstarch

3 tsp xanthan gum

Notes: Gluten-free baking can be made easier and more efficient if you make up a large batch of the flour mixture, sift ingredients together, then freeze in a plastic storage bag or tightly sealed plastic container.

Mung bean flour is available at Asian grocery stores and is a wonderful addition to the light-textured dessert recipes. Chick pea flour is also "light" in texture. Garbanzo bean flour, found in health food stores and some grocery stores, is a bit heavier, but a nice addition for denser desserts, like fruit cakes and sweet breads.

Xanthan gum, despite its intimidating name, is a white powder sold in health food stores, near the flours, that helps to bind the baked good and keep it from crumbling.

As a general rule, when converting favorite recipes into gluten-free masterpieces, use the following measurements of xanthan gum per each cup of gluten-free flour:

Cookies ¼ tsp   Bread 1–1½ tsp
Cakes ½ tsp   Pizza crust 2 tsp
Muffins/quick breads ¾ tsp

GF baking mix

Ingredients

2 1/3 cups chickpea (garbanzo
  bean) flour
2/3 cup cornstarch
1/4 cup sugar

1 1/2 tsp salt
3 1/2 tsp xanthan gum
1 tsp cream of tartar

Instructions

* Combine all ingredients. Store in an airtight container.

Notes: Substitute this mix cup for cup for wheat flour except in bread recipes.

Look for xanthan gum next to the specialty flours.

CHAPTER 17

Breakfast Items

French toast

Ingredients

8 slices of gluten-free bread
4 eggs, beaten well
canola oil for griddle

Instructions

- Heat griddle, grease with canola oil.
- Dip and soak each slice of bread in the beaten eggs.
- Place slices of bread onto hot griddle until brown and crispy on one side. Flip and brown the other side until crispy.
- Serve with maple syrup.

Applesauce pancakes

Ingredients

1½ cup rice flour
2 tbsp potato starch flour
3 tbsp cornstarch
1½ tsp baking powder
½ tsp salt

1 cup rice milk
1 cup applesauce
3 tbsp CF margarine, melted
2 eggs
1 tsp lemon juice

Instructions

- Mix together flours, starches, baking powder and salt.
- In a separate bowl, mix the remaining ingredients.
- Combine both bowls.
- Stir to remove the lumps and cook on a griddle as usual.

Blueberry muffins

Ingredients

½ cup sugar
1¾ cups white rice flour
1½ tsp salt
1 cup water
¾ cup rice milk
2 eggs

½ cup canola oil
2 cups baby rice cereal (like Beechnut)
½ tsp xanthan gum
1 tbsp + 2 tsp baking powder
1 cup blueberries (may use fresh or frozen)

Instructions

- Combine sugar, flour and salt. Add water, milk, eggs and canola oil, and mix well.

- Stir together rice cereal, xanthan gum and baking powder, add to the above mixture. Mix well and gently fold in blueberries.

- Fill sprayed or papered muffin tins until almost full, and bake at 400°F, 200°C, until golden, 20–25 minutes.

Breakfast coffee cake

Ingredients

¾ cup sugar
2 large eggs
⅓ cup mayonnaise
¼ cup soy flour
½ cup rice flour
¼ cup potato starch flour
½ tsp xanthan gum

I tsp cinnamon
I tsp baking powder
¼ tsp baking soda
2 cups chopped apples
½ cup chopped walnuts
  (optional)

Instructions

- Preheat oven to 350°F, 180°C.
- Grease a 9 x 9 inch cake pan and dust with rice flour.
- In a mixing bowl, beat together sugar, eggs, and mayonnaise.
- Whisk together the flours, xanthan gum, cinnamon, baking powder, baking soda, apples, and nuts.
- Spread batter into the prepared pan.
- Bake until cake feels firm when touched in the center and edges begin to pull from pan, about 45 minutes.

Waffles

Ingredients

1 cup GF baking mix
1 tbsp sugar
1 tbsp baking powder
1 tsp xanthan gum
¼ tsp salt

2 cups soymilk (may need to use more if batter is too stiff)
3 tbsp canola oil
1 large egg

Instructions

- Set waffle iron at 4½. Mix all ingredients together, pour into waffle iron.

- Serve with CF margarine and fresh berries or 100% pure maple syrup. This recipe makes about 6 waffles.

- Leftover waffles freeze well – I have used 2 waffles as "bread" for sandwiches. I have also baggied them for brown bag snacks.

Fried potatoes

Ingredients

5 potatoes, washed, peeled
and cut up into small
cubes

canola oil or olive oil
salt
pepper

Instructions

- Boil potatoes in water until cooked all the way through. Stab them with a fork to tell if they are done. Drain.
- Heat oil in pan over medium high heat on stovetop. Add potatoes and pan fry until brown and crispy on the outside. Add salt and pepper to taste.

Mini quiches

Ingredients

1 pack (10oz/275g) frozen
   chopped spinach
4 eggs
¼ cup diced onions

¼ cup diced green bell
   peppers
3 drops hot pepper sauce
   (optional)

Instructions

- Microwave the spinach for 2½ minutes on high. Drain the excess liquid. Line a 12-cup muffin pan with foil baking cups. Spray the cups with cooking spray.

- Combine the eggs, onions, peppers and spinach in a bowl. Mix well. Divide evenly among the muffin cups. Bake at 350°F, 180°C, for 20 minutes, until a knife inserted in the center comes out clean.

Note: Quiche cups can be frozen and reheated in the microwave. Any combination of vegetables can be used, for example, grated carrots, or zucchini or vegetables may be omitted altogether, (except for the spinach).

CHAPTER 18

Breading

Basic GF breading

Ingredients

any kind of crunchy rice cereal (finely ground in blender or food processor)

mashed potato flakes (no sulfites, organic is best)

any kind of crunchy rice crackers (finely ground in blender or food processor)

Instructions

- Mix together equal amounts of the three ingredients. Make a large batch and store in an airtight container, as this breading can be used in other recipes.

CHAPTER 19

Main Dishes

Chicken and dumplin's

Ingredients

Stew:
One 3lb (1.35kg) broiler-fryer
2 quarts (2.3l) water
1 tsp salt
½ tsp pepper

Dumplings:
2 cups buckwheat flour
1 tbsp cornstarch
4 tsp baking powder
1 tsp salt
¼ tsp pepper
¾ cup soy milk
1 egg
3 tbsp cooking oil

Instructions

- Place chicken in a Dutch oven; add water and 1 tsp salt. Bring to a boil; cover, reduce heat, and simmer for 1 hour or until tender. Remove chicken and let it cool slightly. Remove bones and skin from chicken, cutting meat into bite-size pieces; set aside. Bring broth to a boil; add pepper, reduce heat to simmer.

- Combine buckwheat flour, cornstarch, baking powder, salt and pepper; sift together into bowl. Combine soy milk, egg and oil; beat. Add to dry ingredients; stir just until dry ingredients are moistened. Drop tablespoonfuls of mixture into simmering stew. Cover pan tightly. Cook for about 15 minutes without lifting cover.

- Stir in chicken.

Sweet potato pancakes

Ingredients

4 cups canned sweet
   potatoes, drained and
   mashed
½ cup grated sweet onion
3 tbsp lemon juice
1 tsp salt

black pepper to taste
6 egg whites
⅓ cup GF flour mixture I
1 tsp xanthan gum

Instructions

- Combine all ingredients and mix well.
- Heat a small amount of canola oil in a skillet until it is very hot. (A drop of water will sizzle and spit upon contact.)
- Use a spoon to form thin pancakes, pat the batter down to get them as thin as possible. Fry on both sides until brown.
- Add more oil if necessary.
- Serve hot, plain or with applesauce.

Noreen's spicy chicken chili

Ingredients

3 boneless skinless chicken
  breasts
olive oil for sautéing
2 Mayan sweet onions
3 tbsp minced garlic

3 tbsp canned jalepeno
  peppers
1 small can green chilis
2 cans chicken broth
1/4 cup plus 1 tbsp potato
  starch flour

Instructions

- Boil chicken breasts and shred into bite size pieces, set aside.

- Sauté onions, garlic, jalepeno peppers and green chilis in olive oil. In slow cooker, add 2 cans chicken broth and flour, stir until smooth.

- Add cooked chicken, and sautéed veggies, stir. Cook 2–3 hours on high or 5 hours on low.

Tortilla pizza

Ingredients

four 6 inch corn tortillas
6 oz (175g) can tomato paste
dried basil
dried oregano

garlic powder
GFCF cheese slices –
    mozzarella flavor
sliced pepperoni

Instructions

- Place 4 tortillas on cookie sheet or baking stone. Spread tomato paste on tortillas. Sprinkle spices.
- Lay cheese on top, and place 3–4 pepperoni slices on top of cheese.
- Bake at 450°F, 230°C, for about 10 minutes or until cheese is melted.
- Of course you may use any topping you like!

Meatloaf

Ingredients

1 lb (450g) lean ground beef
1 tsp salt
1 egg
½ tsp garlic powder

2 tbsp diced onion
1 cooked medium potato,
   mashed
2 tsp prepared horseradish

Instructions

- Mix all ingredients together in a large bowl. Form into an 8 inch loaf pan. Bake at 350°F, 180°C, for about 1 hour.

Chicken stuffed green peppers

This recipe is from my good friends, Jim and Elizabeth Whelan.

Ingredients

1 onion chopped very fine
1 stalk of celery chopped
   very fine
3 whole carrots, shredded
1 tsp olive oil
1 lb (450g) ground chicken
salt, pepper, garlic powder,
   paprika to taste

2 cups steamed rice
1 can diced tomatoes
4 whole peppers, green,
   yellow, red or any
   combination of these 3
   colors
a little bit of tomato sauce
4 slices of soy or rice cheese

Instructions

- Sauté onion, celery and carrot in olive oil until onion is translucent. Add ground chicken and spices. Continue cooking until chicken is no longer pink. Add cooked rice and mix together thoroughly. Add diced tomatoes with juice. Cook on low over the stove for about 5 minutes so all the flavors can mix.

- While the chicken mixture is cooking, cut the tops off the peppers and steam them in a pan with 2 inches of water on the bottom. Place peppers in baking dish, stuff with chicken mixture, add some tomato sauce on top, and place a slice of soy or rice cheese on top of the tomato sauce. Bake at 350°F, 180°C, or until the cheese is melted.

Note: You may add cumin and hot pepper if you want the meat to be spicy – optional. You can also add a can of corn when you mix in the rice – for more flavor and crunch (translate fiber).

Pad Thai shrimp (or chicken or beef) with peanuts

Ingredients

8 oz (225g) rice noodles
¼ cup smooth peanut butter
3 cups chicken stock
1 lb (450g) raw shrimp peeled and deveined (or chunks of chicken or beef or any combination of all 3)
8 oz (225g) bean sprouts

1 bunch (about 1 cup) green onions, trimmed, cut in 2 inch long pieces
2 tbsp vegetable oil, divided
1 large egg
1 large onion, sliced
⅓ cup chopped peanuts
1 lime, cut into 4 wedges

Instructions

- Bring 5 cups water to boil. Remove from heat and add noodles to hot water. Let stand 7–8 minutes, stirring occasionally until soft and tender. Drain well; set aside.

- Bring chicken stock to a boil. Turn off heat. One tablespoon at a time, thin peanut butter with the stock until it can be poured. Set aside.

- Blanch shrimp 30 seconds in large pot of boiling salted water. Pan fry chicken/beef pieces in a bit of oil in a pan. Add sprouts and green onions, blanch for 5 seconds. Drain and set aside.

- Heat oil in stir-fry pan on High until a drop of water sizzles. Add egg, cook, scrambling it, just until set. Set aside. Wipe out pan with paper towel.

- Coat sides of stir-fry pan; tilt pan to distribute evenly. Heat oil in pan on High. Add onion slices; stir fry 2 minutes.

- Add rice noodles and peanut sauce. Cook, gently stirring, 2–3 minutes until noodles are tender.

- Add shrimp, meat, vegetables, and egg to pan; mix thoroughly. Top each serving with chopped peanuts and a lime wedge.

Chicken curry

Ingredients

2 boneless skinless chicken
  breasts
I cup coarsely chopped
  apple, divided
I small onion
3 tbsp raisins
I tsp curry powder
I clove garlic, minced
¼ tsp ground ginger

⅓ cup water
I ½ tsp GFCF chicken
  bouillon granules
I ½ tsp potato starch
¼ cup coconut milk
½ tsp cornstarch
½ cup uncooked white rice
green onions for garnish

Instructions

- Combine chicken, ¾ cup apple, onion, raisins, curry powder, garlic and ginger in crock-pot.

- Combine water, chicken bouillon granules and potato starch in small bowl; stir until dissolved.

- Add to crock-pot. Cover and cook on Low 3½–4 hours or until onions are tender and chicken is no longer pink. Combine coconut milk and cornstarch in large bowl. Turn off crock-pot; remove insert to heatproof surface. Drain all cooking liquid from chicken mixture and stir into coconut mixture. Add back to insert; stir well. Place insert back in slow cooker. Cover and let stand 5–10 minutes or until sauce is heated through.

- Meanwhile, cook rice according to package directions.

- Serve chicken curry over rice; garnish with remaining ¼ cup apple, and green onions.

Red potato and chicken salad

Ingredients

3 lb (1.35kg) red potatoes
    cooked and quartered
12 oz (350g) chicken breasts
    – cooked
1 small jar pimentos –
    drained
½ cup black olives sliced
⅓ cup scallions sliced

⅓ cup olive oil
3 tbsp red wine vinegar
1 tbsp coarse grain mustard
1 tsp minced garlic
dash of salt
dash of pepper
1½ tsp fresh dill

Instructions

- Combine potatoes, chicken, pimentos, olives and scallions in a large bowl.

- Whisk together olive oil, vinegar, mustard, garlic, salt, pepper and dill.

- Pour dressing over salad and toss.

Scallops with ginger sauce

Ingredients

3 tsp roasted sesame oil, divided

4 (1 inch) diagonally cut green onions

1 ½ lbs (700g) medium sea scallops

¼ tsp salt, divided

¼ cup mirin (sweet rice wine)

¼ cup fish sauce

4 tbsp GF soy sauce

½ tsp grated fresh ginger

¼ tsp crushed red pepper

1 tsp water

½ tsp cornstarch

Instructions

- Heat 1 teaspoon sesame oil in a large cast-iron or heavy skillet over high heat. Add onions; sauté 1 minute or until wilted. Remove from pan; set aside.

- Add remaining 2 tsp sesame oil to pan. Pat scallops dry with paper towels; sprinkle with ⅛ tsp salt. Add scallops; reduce heat to medium, and cook 1 minute or until scallops are done. Remove scallops from pan; keep warm.

- Add mirin, fish sauce, GF soy sauce, ginger, red pepper, and remaining ⅛ tsp salt to pan; bring to a boil. Reduce heat, and simmer 3 minutes. Combine 1 tsp water and cornstarch, stir into sauce. Cook 30 seconds or until sauce begins to thicken. Add scallops to pan; toss to coat.

- Top with onions.

- Yield: 4 servings.

Note: The key to getting a good brown crust is to pat the scallops dry before cooking, sear them in a very hot cast-iron skillet, and, while they cook, only move them to turn them over. Serve over rice noodles.

Grilled flank steak and mixed greens salad

Ingredients

I lb (450g) flank steak
cooking spray

Marinade for steak:

2½ tbsp chopped green
    onions
2 tbsp GF soy sauce
2 tsp rice wine vinegar

½ tsp sugar
2 tsp minced fresh ginger
2 tsp minced garlic cloves

Dressing:

I tbsp GF soy sauce
I tbsp rice wine vinegar
2½ tsp sesame oil

2 tsp miso (soybean paste)
½ tsp sugar

Salad:

8 cups salad greens
2 tomatoes, chopped

I cucumber, seeds removed,
    chopped
2 tsp sesame seeds, toasted

Instructions

- To prepare steak: combine onions, 2 tbsp soy sauce, 2 tsp vinegar, sugar, minced ginger and garlic in a large zip-top plastic bag. Add steak to bag; seal. Marinate in refrigerator I hour, turning occasionally.

- Prepare grill.

- Remove steak from bag. Place steak on grill rack coated with cooking spray; cook 5 minutes on each side or until desired degree of doneness. Let stand 5 minutes. Cut steak diagonally across grain into thin slices. Place steak in a medium bowl. Drizzle with half of dressing; toss well.

- To prepare dressing, combine ingredients in a bowl, stirring well with a whisk until smooth. Set aside.

- Place salad greens in a large bowl. Drizzle with remaining dressing; toss well. Place about 1 cup salad mixture on each of 4 plates. Top each serving with 3 oz (75g) steak, tomato, and cucumber. Sprinkle each serving with ½ tsp sesame seeds.

Southwestern stuffed acorn squash

Ingredients

3 acorn squash
5 oz (150g) of bulk turkey
    sausage or 6 oz (175g) of
    links and remove meat
    from casings
1 small onion, chopped
½ medium red bell pepper,
    chopped
1 clove garlic, minced

1 tbsp chili powder
1 tsp ground cumin
1 can stewed tomatoes,
    chopped up
1 can black beans, rinsed
½ tsp salt
several dashes hot red
    pepper sauce, to taste

Instructions

- Preheat oven to 375°F, 190°C. Lightly coat a large baking sheet with cooking spray.

- Cut squash in half horizontally. Scoop out and discard seeds. Place the squash cut-side down on the prepared baking sheet. Bake until tender, about 45 minutes.

- Meanwhile, lightly coat a large skillet with cooking spray; heat over medium heat. Add turkey sausage and cook, stirring and breaking up with a wooden spoon, until lightly browned, 3–5 minutes. Add onion and bell pepper; cook, stirring often, until softened, 3–5 minutes. Stir in garlic, chili powder and cumin; cook for 30 seconds. Stir in tomatoes, beans, salt and hot sauce, scraping up any browned bits. Cover, reduce heat, and simmer 10 minutes.

- When the squash are tender, reduce oven temperature to 325 °F, 170 °C, fill the squash halves with the turkey mixture. Place on the baking sheet and bake until the filling is heated through, 8–10 minutes.

Citrus glazed salmon

Ingredients

2 lb (900g) fresh or frozen
    salmon fillet, skin
    removed
salt and ground back pepper
¾ cup orange marmalade
2 green onions, sliced
1 clove garlic, minced

2 tsp dry white wine
1 tsp grated fresh ginger
1 tsp Dijon style mustard
¼ tsp cayenne pepper
3 tbsp sliced almonds, toasted

Instructions

- Thaw fish if frozen. Preheat oven to 450°F, 230°C. Rinse fish; pat dry with paper towels. Measure thickest portion of fillet; season with salt and pepper. Place in a shallow baking pan; set aside.

- In a small bowl stir together marmalade, green onions, garlic, wine, ginger, mustard and cayenne pepper. Spoon mixture over salmon.

- Bake, uncovered, for 4–6 minutes per ½ inch thickness or until salmon flakes easily when tested with a fork. Transfer fish and glaze to a serving dish with a lip. Sprinkle with almonds.

- Serve with steamed asparagus, if desired.

Grilled salmon

Salmon is complimented well with delicate flavors such as lemon and dill. Its richness also stands up to robust flavors like teriyaki sauce, and ginger with lime juice. In each case, part of the marinade is reserved and becomes a sauce.

Start with 1 lb (450g) of salmon fillet (with skin on). Cut salmon into 4 portions, place in a shallow glass dish.

Choose one of the marinades/sauces below:

Lemon-dill marinade:

Ingredients

3 tbsp extra-virgin olive oil
3 tbsp lemon juice
1 tbsp chopped fresh dill
2 cloves garlic, minced

$\frac{1}{8}$ tsp salt
freshly ground pepper to taste

Instructions

- Whisk olive oil, lemon juice, dill, garlic, salt and pepper in a small bowl. Use 2 tbsp of the mixture to marinate the salmon. Cover and marinate in the refrigerator for 30 minutes. Serve the remaining mixture as a sauce.

Asian marinade:

Ingredients

3 tbsp GF soy sauce
2 tbsp orange juice
1 tbsp sugar
1 tbsp dry sherry
1 tsp sesame oil

1 clove garlic minced
1 ½ tsp minced fresh ginger
1 tbsp chopped scallion
2 tsp toasted sesame seeds

Instructions

- Whisk GF soy sauce, orange juice, sugar, sherry, sesame oil, garlic and ginger together in a small bowl. Use 2 tbsp of the soy sauce mixture to marinate the salmon. Cover and marinate in the refrigerator for 30 minutes.

- Meanwhile, stir scallions, and sesame seeds into the remaining soy sauce mixture for sauce.

Creamy ginger marinade:

Ingredients

⅓ cup plain soy yogurt
4 tsp minced fresh ginger
2 cloves minced garlic
2 tbsp canola oil
2 tbsp lime juice
1 tbsp honey

⅛ tsp salt
fresh ground pepper to taste
½ cup chopped fresh mint
1 tbsp chopped scallions

Instructions

- Whisk soy yogurt, ginger, garlic, canola oil, lime juice, honey, salt, and pepper in a small bowl.

- Use 2 tbsp of the yogurt mixture to marinate the salmon. Cover and marinate in the refrigerator for 30 minutes. Meanwhile, stir mint and scallion into the remaining yogurt mixture for sauce.

Instructions to grill the salmon

- While the salmon marinates, heat grill to medium-high. Just before cooking, lightly oil grill rack. Place salmon pieces, skin side up, on grill. Close lid and cook for 4 minutes.

- Carefully turn salmon pieces over; cook 4–8 minutes depending on thickness, until opaque in the center and fish flakes when tested with a fork.

- Serve the salmon with the sauce and lemon or lime wedges.

Gluten-free spaghetti

Ingredients

2 tbsp potato starch flour
⅓ cup tapioca flour
⅓ cup cornstarch
1 tbsp xanthan gum

½ tsp salt
2 large eggs
1 tbsp vegetable oil

Instructions

- Combine flours, cornstarch, xanthan gum, and salt. Beat eggs lightly and add oil. Pour egg into flour mixture and stir. Work dough into a firm ball. Knead a minute or two.

- Place ball of dough into your pasta machine. Crank out your spaghetti; you may need to flour your hands with cornstarch or potato flour. This gets very sticky.

- Boil water over the stove, add oil and salt. Cook spaghetti for 10 minutes.

Note: if you don't have a pasta machine, you can roll the dough out until it is very thin and cut it into noodles.

Meatballs

Ingredients

1 lb (450g) lean ground beef	½ tsp garlic powder
1 tsp salt	2 tbsp diced onion
1 egg	

Instructions

- Preheat oven to 350°F, 180°C.
- Combine all ingredients in a large bowl with your hands and roll into bite size balls.
- Place meatballs in a oiled baking pan and bake in preheated oven for about 35 minutes. Add to sauce.

Peanut butter and banana on a corn tortilla

Ingredients

6 inch corn tortillas
peanut butter
bananas

Instructions

- Spread peanut butter on a corn tortilla.
- Put a banana in the center.
- Roll tortilla around the banana. Eat and enjoy!

Peanut butter and jelly sandwich

Ingredients

GF bread
peanut butter
jelly

Instructions

- Start with 2 slices of bread. Smear peanut butter on 1 slice of bread, and jelly on the other. Put the 2 slices of bread together. Ah!

You Americans may think I am crazy for including the most basic sandwich in the world in this cookbook (we in America learn to make these ourselves at age four when Mommy is taking a nap or we don't want what the rest of the family is eating for dinner). But, I have discovered that our friends in the United Kingdom do not know about this sandwich, have never made one and/or have never eaten one.

Chicken nuggets

Ingredients

boneless, skinless chicken
    breast
eggs
fine yellow cornmeal
potato starch
puffed rice cereal ground
    finely in coffee grinder

dried parsley
salt
pepper
onion powder
garlic powder
canola oil for frying

Instructions

- Cut chicken breasts into nuggets.
- Beat a couple of eggs in a small bowl.
- Combine equal amounts of cornmeal, potato starch, rice cereal and seasoning in shallow dish or pan to make coating mix.
- Dip chicken chunks in egg, then dredge in coating mix.
- Fry in hot oil until brown.

Turkey chili

Ingredients

1–2 lb (450–900g) of ground turkey
1 tbsp olive oil
1 large onion chopped
4–5 cloves of garlic, minced
1 tbsp chili powder
2 tsp cumin
2 tsp oregano

2 cans (2 pints/1.2l) chopped tomatoes
3 cans beans (3 pints/1.7l) – I like to mix kidney beans, small white beans and chick peas (garbanzo beans)
1 tsp salt

Instructions

- Brown turkey in oil and drain any fat off.
- Sauté onion and garlic in oil.
- Mix all ingredients together and simmer on the stove for about 40 minutes.

Chili

Ingredients

1 lb (450g) ground beef
1 clove garlic, minced
1 large onion, chopped
1 green pepper, chopped
4 tbsp chili powder
1 tbsp cider vinegar
¼ tsp allspice
¼ tsp coriander

1 tsp cumin
½ tsp salt
½ cup water
2 16 oz (450g) cans of
   crushed tomatoes
2 16 oz (450g) cans of kidney
   beans

Instructions

- Cook beef, garlic, onion and green pepper in skillet over medium heat. Add remaining ingredients.

- Cover, reduce heat, and simmer for 45 minutes. Stir frequently.

Sweet and sour stir fry

Ingredients

1 lb (450g) of boneless cubed chicken (can use beef or sea scallops)
1 tbsp canola or olive oil
1 green pepper cut into strips
1 red pepper cut into strips
1 tbsp cornstarch

¼ cup GF soy sauce
½ pint (275ml) can chunk pineapple in juice
3 tbsp vinegar
3 tbsp brown sugar
½ tsp ground ginger
½ tsp garlic powder

Instructions

- Heat oil in large skillet.
- Cook chicken, stirring frequently until well browned. Add peppers, cook and stir 1–2 minutes.
- Mix cornstarch and soy sauce in a small bowl. Add to pan along with pineapple and juice, vinegar, sugar, ginger and garlic powder. Bring to full boil. Serve with brown rice.

Pizza crust

Ingredients

2 large eggs
¼ cup water
⅓ cup rice flour
⅓ cup potato starch flour

⅓ cup cornstarch
¼ tsp xanthan gum
1 tsp salt
¼ cup shortening, melted

Instructions

- Beat the eggs and water together. Add the flours, cornstarch, xanthan gum and salt. Mix in the melted shortening.

- Spread into a greased 9 × 13 inch pan or shape into a 12 inch circle about ¼ inch thick on a cookie sheet or pizza pan, leaving a thicker crust around the outside of the circle.

- Spread sauce evenly over the unbaked crust and top with your favorite toppings.

- Bake in a preheated 400°F, 200°C, oven for about 25 minutes.

Fried rice

Ingredients

sesame oil
2 eggs well beaten
1 small onion, chopped
4 cloves garlic, minced
5 cups cooked white rice

GF soy sauce
½ package frozen peas and
    carrots
brown sugar

Instructions

- Heat sesame oil over medium heat in large skillet or wok.
- Fry eggs in oil – remove from pan, set aside.
- Add more sesame oil to pan and heat over medium heat.
- Sauté onion and minced garlic in pan.
- Add rice. Add GF soy sauce to taste.
- Add peas and carrots, stir until vegetables are heated through. Add brown sugar to sweeten if desired.

Spice-rubbed London broil

Ingredients

1½ tbsp firmly packed light
   brown sugar
2½ tsp ground coriander
2 tsp minced garlic
2 tsp olive oil

1½ tsp chili powder
½ tsp black pepper
½ tsp ground ginger
½ tsp salt
3 lb (1.35kg) London broil
   steak

Instructions

- Preheat grill to medium.

- Combine the brown sugar, coriander, garlic, olive oil, chili powder, black pepper, ground ginger, and salt in a small bowl and mix well.

- Rub the brown sugar mixture on both sides of the steak.

- Grill steak 8 inches from heat for 15 minutes, turning once. Cut diagonally across the grain into ¼ inch slices.

Baked ham

Ingredients

2 tbsp brown sugar
1 tsp ground cinnamon
1 tsp ground coriander
¾ tsp ground cumin
½ tsp freshly ground black
    pepper
¼ tsp ground allspice
5 lb (2.25kg) bone-in smoked,
    fully cooked ham half

cooking spray
2 tbsp honey
1 tbsp molasses
1 tbsp orange juice
1tbsp grated orange zest
1 tbsp balsamic vinegar

Instructions

- Preheat oven to 350°F, 180°C.

- Combine first 6 ingredients. Trim fat and rind from ham. Rub ham evenly with sugar mixture. Place ham on a broiler pan coated with cooking spray. Cover loosely with foil. Bake for 1 hour and 15 minutes.

- Combine honey, molasses, juice, zest and vinegar in a small bowl, stirring with a whisk. Remove foil from ham; brush honey mixture over ham. Bake, uncovered, 30 minutes or until a thermometer registers 140°F (60°C). Transfer ham to a platter; let stand 15 minutes before slicing.

The next few recipes are made in a slow cooker. I have a Crock-Pot brand and it is one of the best things that has ever happened to me. I bought it, and cooked my first meal in it, and exclaimed, "Where have you been all my life?" I recommend this kitchen tool highly.

Chicken in wine

Ingredients

3 lb (1.35kg) chicken pieces, breasts and thighs work best
salt
black pepper
2 tbsp canola oil

1 medium onion, sliced
1 can (4 oz/110g) sliced mushrooms, drained
½ cup dry sherry
1 tsp Italian seasoning
hot cooked rice

Instructions

- Rinse chicken parts and pat dry. Season chicken lightly with salt and pepper.

- In skillet, brown chicken pieces in oil; remove with slotted spoon and place in slow cooker. Sauté onion and mushrooms in skillet. Add sherry to skillet and stir, scraping to remove brown particles. Pour contents of skillet into slow cooker over chicken. Sprinkle with Italian seasoning. Cover and cook on Low 8–10 hours or on High 3–4 hours.

- Serve chicken over rice and spoon sauce over top.

Candied Polynesian spareribs

Ingredients

2 lb (900g) lean pork
    spareribs
⅓ cup GF soy sauce
¼ cup cornstarch
1 tbsp ground ginger
1 cup sugar
½ cup cider vinegar
¼ cup water

1 tsp salt
½ tsp salt
½ tsp dry mustard
1 small piece gingerroot or
    1 inch long piece of
    crystallized ginger

Instructions

- Cut spareribs into individual 3 inch pieces.

- Mix soy sauce, cornstarch and ground ginger until smooth; brush mixture over spareribs. Place ribs on rack of broiler pan. Bake in preheated 425°F, 220°C, oven 20 minutes to remove fat; drain.

- Combine remaining ingredients in slow cooker, stir well. Add browned ribs. Cover and cook on Low 8–10 hours or on High 4–5 hours. If desired, brown and crisp in broiler for 10 minutes before serving.

Stuffed cabbage

Ingredients

12 large cabbage leaves
4 cups water
1 lb (450g) lean ground beef
   or lamb
½ cup cooked rice
½ tsp salt
¼ tsp dried thyme leaves

¼ tsp ground nutmeg
¼ tsp ground cinnamon
⅛ tsp black pepper
1 can (6 oz/175g) tomato
   paste
¾ cup water

Instructions

- Wash cabbage leaves. Boil 4 cups water. Turn heat off. Soak leaves in water for 5 minutes. Remove, drain and cool.

- Combine remaining ingredients except tomato paste and ¾ cup water. Place 2 tbsp beef mixture on each cabbage leaf and roll firmly. Stack in slow cooker. Combine tomato paste and ¾ cup water and pour over stuffed cabbage. Cover and cook on Low 8–10 hours.

Thai turkey and rice noodles

Ingredients

1 ½ lb (700g) turkey
    tenderloins, cut into
    ¾ inch pieces
1 red bell pepper, cut into
    short, thin strips
1 ¼ cups chicken broth,
    divided
¼ cup GF soy sauce
3 cloves garlic, minced
¾ tsp red pepper flakes
¼ tsp salt

2 tbsp cornstarch
3 green onions, cut into
    ½ inch pieces
⅓ cup creamy peanut butter
12 oz (350g) hot cooked rice
    noodles
¾ cup peanuts, chopped
¾ cup cilantro, chopped

Instructions

- Place turkey, bell pepper, 1 cup broth, GF soy sauce, garlic, red pepper flakes and salt in slow cooker. Cover and cook on Low 3 hours.

- Mix cornstarch with remaining ¼ cup broth in small bowl until smooth. Turn slow cooker to High. Stir in green onions, peanut butter and cornstarch mixture. Cover and cook 30 minutes or until sauce is thickened and turkey is no longer pink in center. Stir well. Serve over rice noodles. Sprinkle with peanuts and cilantro.

Beef fajitas

Ingredients

1 lb 8 oz (700g) beef flank
  steak
1 cup chopped onion
1 green bell pepper, cut into
  ½ inch pieces
1 tbsp cilantro
2 cloves garlic, minced
1 tsp chili powder
1 tsp cumin

1 tsp ground coriander
½ tsp salt
1 can (8 oz/225g) chopped
  tomatoes
12 corn tortillas

Toppings:
guacamole
salsa

Instructions

- Cut flank steak into 6 portions. In slow cooker, combine steak, onion, bell pepper, cilantro, garlic, chili powder, cumin, coriander and salt. Add tomatoes. Cover and cook on Low 8–10 hours or on High 4–5 hours.

- Remove meat from slow cooker and shred with fork. Return meat to slow cooker and stir. To serve fajitas, spread meat mixture into corn tortillas and top with toppings. Roll up tortillas.

CHAPTER 20

Side Dishes

Cornbread stuffing

Ingredients

I lb (450g) GF cornbread cubes
¼ cup GFCF margarine
I cup celery, chopped
I cup onion, chopped
I tsp thyme, dried

I tsp sage, dried
I cup fresh parsley, chopped
I egg, slightly beaten
I cup GF chicken broth
salt and pepper to taste

Instructions

- Start with bite size cornbread pieces. Place cubes on baking sheet and bake for 30 minutes (or until toasted) at 350°F, 180°C, turn cubes every 10 minutes for even toasting. Remove cornbread cubes from the oven and cool to room temperature.

- Melt GFCF margarine in pan; sauté celery and onion until soft. Stir in the thyme, sage and parsley. Cool. Stir the cornbread and onion-celery mixture together. Add egg and mix well. Add chicken stock and mix lightly but thoroughly. Add salt and pepper to taste. Stuff bird or bake the stuffing in a greased, covered casserole dish at 350°F, 180°C, for 30–35 minutes.

Sweet rice

Ingredients

3 cups cooked rice
3 eggs, slightly beaten
2 apples, peeled and grated
¼ cup raisins

⅓ cup brown sugar
I tsp cinnamon
¼ cup canola oil

Instructions

- Spray a 9 × 9 inch pan with cooking spray.
- Combine all ingredients in a large bowl, mixing well.
- Spread into prepared pan.
- Bake at 350°F, 180°C, for 45–60 minutes, until the top is firm and the edges are light brown.

CHAPTER 21

Soups

Vegetable rice soup with kale

This is an easy soup to make, it is rich in phytochemicals, low in fat, high in fiber and has a delightful peppery taste from the kale.

Ingredients

2 tsp olive oil

2 medium zucchini, quartered lengthwise and sliced ¼ inch thick

10 carrots, chopped

1 medium onion, chopped

2 cups coarsely chopped kale

1 lb 12 oz (800g) of canned diced tomatoes, with basil, garlic and oregano, undrained

4 cups GF vegetable broth

15 oz (425g) can of chick peas, white northern beans, or kidney beans, drained and rinsed

¼ cup brown rice

salt to taste

pepper to taste

Instructions

- Heat oil in a large pot. Add zucchini, carrots and onion; sauté over high heat until onion is transparent, about 7 minutes. Add kale; sauté until wilted, about 3–5 minutes.

- Add diced tomatoes, broth, beans and rice. Simmer until carrots and rice are tender, about 30–40 minutes. Stir in salt and pepper to taste.

Chili chicken stew

Ingredients

7 oz (200g) can chipotle chilis in adobo sauce
1 tsp olive oil
½ cup chopped green onions
1 cup chopped green bell pepper
1 tsp ground cumin
1 tbsp minced garlic

2 cans chicken broth
2 cups chopped cooked chicken
11 oz (325g) can whole-kernel corn, drained
1 can diced tomatoes, undrained
1 small can green chilis, undrained

Instructions

- Remove 1 chili from can; reserve the remaining chilis and sauce for another use. Mince chili.

- Heat the oil in a large saucepan over medium-high heat. Add onions, bell pepper, cumin and garlic; sauté 4 minutes or until the vegetables are soft.

- Stir in minced chilli, broth, chicken, corn, tomatoes and chilis. Bring to a boil. Reduce heat, and simmer 3 minutes.

CHAPTER 22

Salads

Spinach salad

Salad ingredients

fresh baby leaf spinach
mandarin oranges
crumbled bacon

slivered toasted almonds
sliced mushrooms
green onions, sliced

Salad dressing ingredients

¼ tsp garlic powder
1 cup canola oil
½ cup red wine vinegar
½ cup sugar

1 tsp salt
1 tsp dry mustard
4 tbsp poppy seeds

Instructions

- Combine dressing ingredients; stir well and toss over salad ingredients.

Note: The dressing recipe makes more dressing than needed. If you are transporting the dish, add the dressing just before you serve the salad.

Asian coleslaw

Ingredients

½ cup roasted unsalted
   peanuts
3 cups shredded napa
   cabbage
1 cup grated carrots
1 diced small red bell pepper
½ cup chopped scallions
¼ cup mayonnaise

2 tbsp GF soy sauce
4 tsp rice vinegar
1 tbsp brown sugar
1 tbsp toasted sesame oil
1 tsp chili paste with garlic
1 tsp minced fresh ginger
1 minced garlic clove

Instructions

- Toast peanuts in a small, dry skillet over medium-low heat, stirring constantly, until lightly browned and fragrant, 2–3 minutes. Transfer to plate to cool.

- Place cabbage, carrots, red bell pepper and scallions in a large bowl.

- Whisk mayo, soy sauce, rice vinegar, brown sugar, sesame oil, chili paste with garlic, fresh ginger and garlic clove in a small bowl until smooth.

- Add the dressing to the cabbage mixture and toss to coat well. Sprinkle with toasted peanuts.

Green bean salad

Salad ingredients

1 lb (450g) fresh green beans
1 tbsp minced garlic
1 tbsp minced ginger

1 cup chopped green onions
2 tsp red pepper flakes

Salad dressing ingredients

4 tsp dry mustard powder
3 tbsp rice vinegar
2 tbsp GF soy sauce

1 tbsp cold water
2 tsp sugar
2 tsp sesame oil

Instructions

- Trim and cut the green beans into 1 inch lengths. Cook in rapidly boiling water, about 5 minutes or until crunchy–tender.

- Drain beans, immerse in cold water to stop the cooking until they are cool, then drain well.

- Mix the dressing ingredients in a small bowl with a whisk until well blended.

- Toss the green beans with the garlic, ginger, green onion, red pepper flakes and dressing. Serve immediately.

Beet salad

Ingredients

3 cans beets
¼ cup water
¼ cup rice vinegar
¼ cup brown sugar
1 tbsp extra-virgin olive oil

1 tsp dry mustard powder
1 large onion, minced
salt to taste

Instructions

- Drain beets and cut into cubes. Combine the cubed beets in a bowl with the other ingredients, add salt to taste, and chill. Stir several times.
- This salad will keep for a week in the refrigerator.

Chicken sandwich filling

Ingredients

2 boneless skinless chicken breasts –
cooked and cut up into cubes
mayonnaise

salt
pepper

Instructions

- In a large bowl, combine cut-up chicken, mayonnaise, salt and pepper to taste.
- Serve as filling in a sandwich or as a topping on a salad.

Tuna sandwich filling

Ingredients

white albacore tuna fish canned in water
mayonnaise

Instructions

- Drain tuna from can.
- Mix mayonnaise to taste.
- Serve as a filling in a sandwich or on top of a salad for added protein, and the beneficial omega 3 fatty acids.

Egg sandwich filling

Ingredients

4 boiled eggs
mayonnaise

salt
pepper

Instructions

- Boil water in 2 quart pan on top of stove. Gently place one egg at a time in the water with a slotted spoon. Boil for 13 minutes. Drain and cool eggs immediately – run eggs under cold water and then place them in a bowl of ice water until cool. This will prevent them from getting the dark gray sulfur ring that coats the yolk.

- Peel the eggs and cut each one in half. Dump the yolks into a bowl and smash them up. Cut the whites into cubes, and add to the yolks.

- Mix with mayonnaise, add salt and pepper to taste.

- Serve as a filling in a sandwich or on top of a salad for added protein.

CHAPTER 23

Salad Dressings

Tahini dressing

Ingredients

1 cup tahini
½ cup water
juice of 2 lemons, or to taste
3 cloves garlic, minced
1 tbsp minced fresh cilantro,
    or to taste

1 tsp ground coriander
½ tsp ground cumin
salt to taste
ground red pepper to taste

Instructions

- Whisk all ingredients together in a small bowl. Thin with water as necessary, especially when using as a dressing.

- Adjust seasonings to taste.

- Use immediately or cover and refrigerate. This dressing goes well with salads or makes a good dip for fresh veggies.

"Creamy" ranch salad dressing

Ingredients

1 cup mayonnaise
¼ cup plain soy milk
1 ½ tbsp cider vinegar
1 tbsp canola oil
1 tbsp chopped fresh Italian
    parsley

1 clove garlic, chopped
½ tsp salt
¼ tsp pepper

Instructions

- Combine all ingredients in a blender. Blend until well mixed.

CHAPTER 24

Breads

Ginger bread

Ingredients

1 ½ cup flour mix
2 tbsp potato flour
1 tsp salt
1 ½ tsp baking soda
1 tsp cinnamon
1 ½ tsp ginger

½ cup shortening
½ cup sugar
1 egg, beaten
1 cup molasses
¾ cup hot water

Instructions

- Sift together flours, salt, soda, cinnamon and ginger.
- Cream together shortening, sugar and egg. Then add molasses. Alternately add dry mixture and hot water to creamed mixture.
- When mixed to a smooth, thick sour cream-like consistency, pour in greased 8 × 8 inch pan. Bake at 350°F, 180°C, for 35–40 minutes. Check for doneness.

Corn bread

Ingredients

¾ cup pure maple syrup
½ cup canola oil
2 eggs, lightly beaten
1½ cup GF baking mix
3 tsp baking powder

1 tsp xanthan gum
⅛ tsp salt
1½ cups yellow corn meal
1 cup soy milk

Instructions

- Blend together maple syrup and oil, then mix in eggs. In a separate bowl, mix dry ingredients well, then blend them into the egg mixture, alternating with soy milk.

- Bake in a greased loaf pan at 400°F, 200°C, for 30 minutes, or until bread tests done. For muffins, check after 15 minutes.

Note: I made 15 muffins from this recipe and they took 20 minutes to bake – I filled the cups almost full.

Applesauce bread

Ingredients

2 cups GF baking mix

2 tsp xanthan gum

1 tsp cinnamon

½ tsp baking powder

½ tsp baking soda

½ cup GFCF buttery spread

1½ cup sugar

2 eggs, lightly beaten

½ cup applesauce

¼ tsp lemon juice

½ cup soy milk

1 tsp vanilla

½ cup chopped walnuts

Instructions

- Stir together dry ingredients and set aside.

- In large bowl, cream buttery spread and sugar. Add eggs, applesauce and lemon juice.

- Alternately add the dry ingredients and the milk to the applesauce mixture, then stir in vanilla and nuts. Add more applesauce or soy milk if the batter seems too stiff.

- Bake in an oiled 9 × 5 inch loaf pan at 375°F, 190°C, for 50–60 minutes, until bread tests done with a toothpick.

Garlic bread

Ingredients

GF bread
GFCF buttery spread
GF garlic powder

Instructions

- Preheat oven to 350°F, 180°C.

- Lay GF bread on a cookie sheet and spread buttery spread on bread. Sprinkle garlic powder lightly on top.

- Bake in oven for 5–7 minutes, until spread is melted and bread is toasted.

Banana bread

Ingredients

⅓ cup CF margarine
⅔ cup sugar
2 eggs, beaten
1¼ cup GF flour mix
1 tsp lemon rind, grated

1¼ tsp baking powder
½ tsp baking soda
½ tsp salt
3 mashed bananas
½ cup chopped walnuts

Instructions

- Cream margarine with sugar.
- Stir in beaten eggs, blend.
- Mix in the dry ingredients.
- Pour into a greased 5 × 9 inch loaf pan.
- Bake in preheated 350°F, 180°C, oven for 50 minutes.
- Check for doneness.

Indian quick bread

Ingredients

1 cup grated coconut (no sulfites)
1 cup GF baking mix
¾ cup sugar
½ cup potato starch flour
½ cup white rice flour

2 tsp xanthan gum
1 tbsp baking powder
1 cup rice milk
2 eggs, beaten
¼ cup canola oil
1 tsp vanilla

Instructions

- Spread the coconut on a cookie sheet and toast at 350°F, 180°C, until lightly browned. Watch carefully, as coconut burns quickly. It should be light brown – stir once. This will take only 3–5 minutes.

- Combine the coconut with the dry ingredients and mix well.

- In a separate bowl, mix the wet ingredients and add to dry mixture. Blend well and pour into an oiled 9 × 5 × 3 inch loaf pan. Bake at 350°F, 180°C, for 50–60 minutes, until a toothpick inserted comes out clean and the bread is golden brown.

CHAPTER 25

Snacks

Trail mix

Ingredients

almonds	raisins
peanuts	your favorite GFCF dry
cashews	breakfast cereal

Instructions

- Mix all ingredients together and store in airtight container.

Fruit and popcorn bars

Ingredients

9 cups popped popcorn
(remove unpopped
kernels!!)
¾ cup packed brown sugar
¼ cup apple juice
3 tbsp CF margarine

2 tbsp light corn syrup
¼ tsp salt
1 ½ cups dried fruit (may use
raisins, fruit bits,
apricots)
¾ cup peanuts

Instructions

- Grease a very large bowl and set aside.
- Combine brown sugar, apple juice, margarine, corn syrup and salt in a 2–3 quart saucepan. Boil over medium heat, 5–6 minutes, until mixture is slightly thickened.
- Place popcorn, dried fruit and peanuts in greased bowl.
- Immediately drizzle hot sugar mixture over popcorn and fruit, stirring quickly with a wooden spoon.
- With greased hands, quickly press mixture into 9 × 13 inch pan. Cool.
- Cut into single serving size bars and wrap in plastic wrap.

Fresh chickpea hummus

Ingredients

1 can (15 oz/425g) chickpeas
½ cup tahini (sesame paste)
2 tbsp fresh lemon juice
2 tsp olive oil

3 cloves garlic, minced
2 tsp ground cumin
¼ tsp ground red pepper
salt to taste

Instructions

- Drain the chickpeas, reserving ¼ to ½ cup of the liquid.

- Combine the chickpeas, tahini, lemon juice, oil, garlic, cumin, red pepper and salt in a blender or food processor. Puree until smooth, adding the chickpea liquid if needed to thin the puree.

- Refrigerate for 3–4 hours before serving (I usually can't wait this long to eat it!) to blend the flavors.

- Serve with veggies, like cut-up carrots, celery, cut-up red or green peppers, cucumbers, or serve on GFCF crackers.

Papaya-strawberry smoothie

Ingredients

1 cup papaya pieces (fresh or
   frozen)
1 cup strawberries (fresh or
   frozen)
8 oz (225g) vanilla soy yogurt

12 oz (350g) can papaya
   nectar, chilled
crushed ice

Instructions

- Add all ingredients to a blender and blend until smooth. Pour
  into glasses and serve.

Mango-banana smoothie

Ingredients

½ ripe mango, chopped
1 small banana, chopped
1 vanilla soy yogurt

1 cup orange juice
crushed ice

Instructions

- Add all ingredients to a blender and blend until smooth. Pour into glasses and serve.

CHAPTER 26

Desserts

Apple crisp

Ingredients

6 cups apples – peeled and
    sliced
½ cup brown sugar
¼ tsp cinnamon
dash salt

1 cup GF flour mixture
1 cup chopped walnuts
½ cup brown sugar
6 tbsp CF margarine

Instructions

- Mix first 4 ingredients together and spoon into greased 9 ×
  13 inch pan.
- Mix next 4 ingredients together. Crumble over apple mixture.
- Bake uncovered at 350°F, 180°C, for 1 hour.

Berry apple crunch

Ingredients

1 lb (450g) frozen blueberries
1 green apple, cored and
    diced
¼ cup light brown sugar,
    packed
½ tsp almond extract
1½ tbsp cornstarch or
    arrowroot powder
½ cup apple juice

non-stick cooking spray
¼ cup crushed rice cereal
¼ cup brown sugar
¼ cup walnuts, chopped
⅓ cup GF flour mix
3 tbsp light, extra virgin olive
    oil
¼ tsp salt (optional)

Instructions

- Preheat oven to 400°F, 200°C.

- In a bowl, toss together the blueberries, apple, brown sugar and almond extract.

- In a cup, mix the cornstarch and juice, and add to the fruit mixture, stirring well.

- Spray an 8 inch square baking dish with non-stick cooking spray. Pour in the mixture.

- Mix together the remaining ingredients. Crumble the mixture on top of the fruit.

- Bake for 30 minutes. Raise heat to broil and brown topping lightly for 1–2 minutes.

Sponge cake

Ingredients

7 eggs
1 ½ cups sugar, sifted
1 ½ tbsp lemon juice

1 ½ tsp grated lemon rind
¾ cup potato starch, sifted
dash of salt

Instructions

- Separate 6 of the eggs. Beat the 6 yolks and the one whole egg until frothy. Gradually add sifted sugar, lemon juice and lemon rind, beating constantly and thoroughly. Then gradually add sifted potato starch, stirring constantly to ensure thorough blending.

- Beat egg whites with the salt until stiff but not dry. Fold gently but thoroughly into egg yolk mixture.

- Place in ungreased 10 inch tube pan. Bake at 350°F, 180°C, for about 55 minutes or until cake springs back when touched gently with fingers. Invert pan and cool thoroughly before removing cake.

- This cake is light and airy like angel food cake – terrific topped with fruit or as the "shortcake" for your fresh strawberries. It would also work well as the base for a trifle!

White cake

Ingredients

4 egg whites
½ tsp cream of tartar
I level cup shortening
⅔ cup sugar
2 tsp vanilla

4 egg yolks
½ tsp baking powder
½ tsp baking soda
2 level cups tapioca flour

Instructions

- Preheat oven to 350°F, 180°C. Beat together egg whites and cream of tartar until stiff. Set aside.

- Cream shortening and sugar together. Beat in vanilla and egg yolks. Add baking powder, baking soda and tapioca flour. Stir well. Fold in whipped egg whites. Bake in a greased angel food cake pan for 35 minutes or until done.

- Invert pan and tap the cake out of the pan onto a wire rack. Allow to cool.

Marshmallow treats

Ingredients

3 tbsp GFCF margarine
40 marshmallows or 4
   cups mini
   marshmallows

6 cups GFCF cereal (any kind will
   do, experiment with lots of
   different kinds!)
non-stick cooking spray

Instructions

- In a large microwave-safe bowl, melt margarine and marshmallows on high for 2 minutes, stirring after 1 minute.

- Add cereal, stirring until well coated.

- Spray your hands with non-stick cooking spray and spread cereal mixture into a shallow baking pan coated with cooking spray. Let cool.

Dark fudge brownies

Ingredients

15 oz (425g) can unseasoned black beans (no, I am not kidding)

4 oz (110g) unsweetened baking chocolate

1 tbsp CF margarine

6 egg whites

2 cups sugar

3 tbsp GF baking mix

1 tsp xanthan gum

2 tbsp instant coffee powder

½ cup chopped walnuts

non-stick cooking spray

Instructions

- Preheat oven to 350°F, 180°C. Spray a 9 × 13 inch pan with cooking spray. Place the beans in a colander and rinse thoroughly with running water; set aside and drain.

- Place the chocolate and margarine in a small microwavable bowl. Microwave for 60–90 seconds or until very smooth.

- In a food processor or blender, blend the drained beans and 2 egg whites until smooth.

- In a large bowl, combine the bean puree, sugar, GF baking mix, xanthan gum, coffee powder and the remaining 4 egg whites.

- With an electric mixer, beat until well combined. Mix in the melted chocolate.

- Pour the brownie mixture into prepared pan. Sprinkle the walnuts on top of the brownie batter.

- Bake for 35 minutes until the brownie pulls away from the sides of the pan. Cool completely in the pan before cutting into bars.

CHAPTER 27

Cookies

Sugar cookies

Ingredients

1 cup shortening	½ tsp baking powder
1 cup sugar	½ rounded tsp xanthan gum
1 egg	1 pinch salt
2¼ cups GF baking mix	1 tsp vanilla

Instructions

- Preheat oven to 400°F, 200°C.

- Blend shortening and sugar. Add egg, beat until blended.

- Add GF baking mix, baking powder, xanthan gum and salt. Blend until smooth. Add vanilla, blend.

- Cover cookie sheet surface with cornstarch. Pat down dough to ¼ inch thickness. Use cookie cutters to cut into desired shapes. Place cookies on cookie sheet. Bake in preheated oven until lightly browned, about 8–10 minutes.

Ginger snap cookies

Ingredients

1 cup sugar
¾ cup white vegetable
   shortening
1 egg
¼ cup molasses
2 cups GF baking mix
1½ tsp ginger

1 tsp xanthan gum
1 tsp cinnamon
½ tsp baking soda
½ tsp ground mace
½ tsp salt
granulated sugar

Instructions

- Cream sugar and shortening, then add the egg and molasses.

- Sift and combine dry ingredients and add to creamed mixture.

- Roll into walnut sized balls, then dredge in granulated sugar.

- Cookies will spread while they bake so space them 2 inches apart on cookie sheet.

- Bake at 350°F, 180°C, 10–12 minutes for soft, chewy cookies, 13–15 minutes for crispy snaps.

Loretta O's peanut butter cookies

Ingredients

2 cups peanut butter
1 cup sugar
2 or 3 eggs

Instructions

- Mix ingredients together, drop onto cookie sheet. Bake at 350°F, 180°C, for 15–20 minutes.

This recipe was give to me from a friend with celiac disease. She writes, "My grandson loves these – so does his father and mother and the guys at his dad's work. You will never know they are flourless when you eat them!"

Peanut butter cookies

Ingredients

I cup natural peanut butter
    (no sugar added)
¾ cup superfine sugar
I large egg

I tsp baking soda
¼ tsp salt
granulated sugar (for rolling)

Instructions

- Line a baking sheet with parchment paper. Place a rack in the lower third of the oven. Set the oven at 350°F, 180°C.

- In a bowl combine the peanut butter, superfine sugar, egg, baking soda and salt. With a wooden spoon, stir until well mixed.

- Take a tablespoon of dough, form it into a ball, and roll it in granulated sugar. Place the ball on the baking sheet and flatten it with the tines of a fork. Continue shaping the remaining dough.

- Bake the cookies for 10–12 minutes or until lightly brown. Do not overbake.

- Leave the cookies on the sheet until they are almost cool. They are delicate when warm and break easily. Store in an airtight container.

Makes 24 to 26 cookies.

Chocolate chip cookies

Ingredients

1 cup canola oil
¾ cup sugar
¾ cup brown sugar
2 eggs
1 tsp vanilla

2⅓ cups GF baking mix
1 tsp baking soda
1 tsp salt
2 cups CF chocolate chips

Instructions

- Preheat oven to 350°F, 180°C. Grease a baking sheet.
- Combine oil and sugars in a large bowl and beat with a mixer on medium high speed. Add eggs, one at a time, mixing until creamy. Add vanilla.
- Reduce speed to low and gradually add baking mix, baking soda and salt. Stir in chocolate chips.
- Drop onto baking sheet 2 inches apart. Flatten slightly.
- Bake 10–12 minutes. Remove cookies from pan. Cool on wire racks.

Makes about 24.

Yummy peanut butter balls

Ingredients

I cup peanut butter (all natural, nothing but peanuts and salt, mix well in jar, then measure)

¼ cup GF flour mixture I
¼ cup confectioners' sugar
¼ cup cornstarch
½ cup honey

Instructions

- In a mixing bowl, combine all ingredients until a smooth, soft dough is formed. Add more GF flour mixture I, if too oily.

- Roll into I inch balls and refrigerate on parchment paper, or waxed paper.

A Nutritional Table
of GFCF Foods

Vitamin/ Mineral	GFCF food source	Bodily function
Vitamin A	Apricots, asparagus, broccoli, cantaloupe melons, carrots, eggs, green leafy vegetables, pumpkin, spinach, winter squash, sweet potatoes, tomatoes, watermelon	Prevention of night blindness, promotes bone growth, teeth development, helps form and maintain healthy skin, hair, mucous membranes, builds body's resistance to infection
Vitamin C	Broccoli, Brussels sprouts, cabbage, collards, grapefruit, green peppers, kale, lemons, mangos, orange juice, oranges, papayas, potatoes, spinach, strawberries, tangerines, tomatoes, watercress	Aids iron absorption, helps heal wounds, prevents scurvy, promotes healthy capillaries, gums and teeth, helps form collagen in connective tissue, increases calcium absorption, reduces free radical production
Vitamin B12	Beef, clams, eggs, flounder, herring, liverwurst, mackerel, oysters, sardines, snapper	Promotes normal growth and development, necessary for normal DNA synthesis, promotes normal metabolism, cell development, helps manufacture nerve cell covering, maintains normal nervous system function

Vitamin/ Mineral	GFCF food source	Bodily function
Biotin	Almonds, bananas, brown rice, cashew nuts, chicken, clams, eggs, green peas, lentils, mackerel, meat, mushrooms, peanut butter, peanuts, salmon, soybeans, tuna, walnuts	Helps formation of fatty acids, works in metabolism of amino acids and carbohydrates, necessary for normal growth, development and health
Choline	Cabbage, cauliflower, egg yolk, garbanzo beans (chick peas), kale, lentils, peanuts, soybeans	Maintains cell membrane integrity, works in function of nervous system including mood, behavior, orientation, personality traits, judgment
Vitamin D	Cod liver oil, herring, mackerel, salmon, sardines, tuna	Necessary for growth regulation, hardening and repair of bone, promotes strong teeth
Vitamin E	Almonds, asparagus, avocados, brazil nuts, broccoli, canola oil, corn, corn oil, cottonseed oil, hazelnuts, peanuts, peanut oil, safflower oil, soybean oil, spinach, sunflower seeds, walnuts	Promotes normal growth and development, promotes normal red blood cell formation, antioxidant, improves immunity
Folic acid	Asparagus, avocados, bananas, beans, beets, Brussels sprouts, cabbage, cantaloupe melons, citrus fruits and juices, garbanzo beans, green leafy vegetables, lentils, bean sprouts	Normal red blood cell formation, necessary for normal patterns of growth and development, helps in metabolism of amino acids and protein synthesis
Niacin	Chicken (white meat), dried peas, dried beans, halibut, peanut butter, peanuts, pork, potatoes, salmon, soybeans, swordfish, tuna, turkey	Aids in release of energy from foods, helps to synthesize DNA

Vitamin/ Mineral	GFCF food source	Bodily function
Pantothenic acid	Avocados, bananas, broccoli, chicken, collard greens, eggs, lentils, lobster, meats, oranges, peanut butter, peanuts, peas, soybeans, sunflower seeds	Necessary in the process of energy metabolism of carbohydrates, protein and fat
Vitamin K	Alfalfa, asparagus, broccoli, Brussels sprouts, cabbage, green leafy vegetables, seaweed, spinach	Necessary for normal blood clotting
Pyridoxine	Avocados, bananas, chicken, beef, ham, hazelnuts, lentils, potatoes, salmon, shrimp, soybeans, sunflower seeds, tuna	Necessary for protein carbohydrate and fat utilization
Riboflavin	Bananas, eggs, ham, pork, tuna	Needed for normal tissue respiration, works in conjunction with other B vitamins, promotes normal growth and development
Thiamin	Baked potato, garbanzo beans, ham, kidney beans, navy beans, orange juice, oranges, oysters, peanuts, peas, raisins, brown rice	Promotes normal growth and development, necessary for converting carbohydrates into energy in muscles and nervous system
Calcium	Almonds, brazil nuts, broccoli, canned salmon, canned sardines, tofu, turnip greens	Necessary for normal activity of nervous, muscular and skeletal systems, builds bones and teeth, maintains bone density and strength, helps regulate heartbeat, blood clotting, muscle contraction, promotes normal growth and development, promotes storage and release of some body hormones

Vitamin/ Mineral	GFCF food source	Bodily function
Copper	Avocados, fish, legumes, lentils, lobster, nuts, oysters, peanuts, raisins, salmon, shellfish, soybeans, spinach	Promotes normal red blood cell formation, assists in production of several enzymes involved in respiration, promotes normal insulin function
Iodine	Lobster, oysters, salmon, salted nuts, seeds, saltwater fish like cod, haddock and herring, sea salt, seaweed, shrimp and iodized table salt	Promotes normal function of thyroid gland, keeps skin, hair, nails healthy
Iron	Egg yolk, fish, garbanzo beans, lentils, blackstrap molasses, mussels, oysters, red meat, seaweed, green leafy vegetables	Helps in the process of getting oxygen to all parts of the body, helps muscles get extra energy when they work hard
Magnesium	Almonds, avocados, bananas, bluefish, carp, cod, green leafy vegetables, flounder, halibut, herring, mackerel, molasses, nuts, ocean perch, shrimp, swordfish	Activates essential enzymes, affects metabolism of protein, helps to transport sodium and potassium across cell membranes, influences calcium levels inside cells, aids muscle contractions
Manganese	Beans, blueberries, blackberries, buckwheat, carrots, hazelnuts, peanuts, peas, pecans, seaweed, spinach, tea	Promotes normal growth and development, promotes nerve function, helps promote blood clotting
Molybdenum	Beans, green leafy vegetables, lean meats, peas, legumes	Promotes normal growth and development, aids in elimination of waste in urine

Vitamin/ Mineral	GFCF food source	Bodily function
Phosphorus	Almonds, beans, eggs, fish, peanuts, peas, poultry, canned sardines, scallops, soybeans, sunflower seeds, tuna	Helps in the utilization of B-complex vitamins, works with calcium to build strong bones and teeth, promotes energy metabolism, promotes growth, maintenance and repair of all body tissues
Potassium	Asparagus, avocados, bananas, beans, cantaloupe melons, carrots, citrus fruit, citrus juices, tomato juice, molasses, nuts, parsnips, potatoes, raisins, canned sardines, spinach	Promotes regular heartbeat, promotes normal muscle contraction, maintains water balance in body, maintains normal function of brain, skeletal muscles and kidneys
Selenium	Broccoli, brown rice, cabbage, chicken, garlic, mushrooms, onions, seafood, tuna	Works as an antioxidant, promotes normal growth and development
Sodium	Bacon, clams, green beans, ham, olives, pickles, salted nuts, canned sardines, table salt, canned tomatoes	Helps regulate water balance in body, plays crucial role in maintaining normal blood pressure, aids in muscle contraction and nerve transmission
Zinc	Lean beef, egg yolk, fish, herring, lamb, maple syrup, blackstrap molasses, oysters, pork, sesame seeds, soybeans, sunflower seeds, turkey	Promotes normal growth and development, aids wound healing, maintains normal taste and sense of smell, helps in process of moving CO_2 out of tissues to lungs

Source: Pennington and Douglas 2004.

Further Reading

Books

Agatston, A. (2003) *The South Beach Diet.* New York: Random House.

Feingold, B. (1975) *Why Your Child is Hyperactive.* New York: Random House.

Hagman, B. (2000) *The Gluten-Free Gourmet.* New York: Henry Holt and Company, LLC (original work published 1990).

Lewis, L. (1998) *Special Diets for Special Kids.* Arlington, Texas: Future Horizons, Inc.

Pennington, J.A.T. and Douglas, J.S. (2004) *Bowes and Church's Food Values of Portions Commonly Used,* 18th edition. Philadelphia: Lippincott (original work published 1937).

Rapp, D. (1992) *Is This Your Child?* New York: HarperPaperbacks.

Reichenberg-Ullman, J. and Ullman, R. (1996) *Ritalin-Free Kids.* Rocklin, CA: Prima Publishing.

Seroussi, K. (2002) *Unraveling the Mystery of Autism and Pervasive Developmental Disorder: A Mother's Story of Research and Recovery.* New York: First Broadway Books (original work published 2000: Simon & Schuster).

Journal articles

D'Eufemia, P., Celli, M., Finocchiaro, R., Pacifico, L., *et al.* (1996) 'Abnormal intestinal permeability in children with autism.' *Acta Pediatrica 85,* 1076–1079.

Horvath K., Papadimitriou, J., Rabsztyn, A., Drachenberg, C. and Tildon, J.T. (1999) 'Gastrointestinal abnormalities in children with autistic disorder.' *J Pediatr 135,* 559–563.

Knivsberg, A.-M., Wiig, K., Lind, G., Nodland, M. and Reichelt, L. (1990) 'Dietary interventions in autistic syndromes.' *Brain Dysfunction 3* (5–6), 315–327.

Knivsberg, A.-M., Reibhelt, K., Nodland, M. and Lind, G. (1994) 'Probable etiology and possible treatment of childhood autism.' *Brain Dysfunction 4*, 308–319.

Reichelt, K, Ekrem, J. and Scott, H. (1990) 'Gluten, milk proteins and autism: Dietary intervention effects on behavior and peptide secretion.' *Journal of Applied Nutrition 42*, 1–11.

Rowe, K. *et al.* (1988) 'Synthetic food colourings and hyperactivity; a double-blind crossover study.' *Austrialia Paediatric Journal, 24*, 2, 143–147.

Rowe, K.S. and Rowe, K.J. (1994) 'Synthetic food coloring and behavior; a dose response effect in a double blind, placebo-controlled, repeated-measures study.' *Journal of Pediatrics 125*, 691–698.

Shattock, P., Kennedy, A., Rowell, F. and Berney, T. (1990) 'Role of neuropeptides in autism and their relationships with classical neurotransmitter.' *Brain Dysfunction 3*, 328.

Weiss, B., Williams, J.H., Margens, S., Abrams, B., *et al.* (1980) 'Behavioral responses to artificial food colors.' *Science*, March, 28, *207*, 4438, 1487–1489.

Government papers

US Department of Health and Human Services (2005) Public Health Service, National Toxicology Program Pursuant to Section 301(b) (4) of the Public Health Service Act as Amended by Section 262, PL 95–622 *Official Citation: Report on Carcinogens*, eleventh Edition.

United States Department of Agriculture (2005a) *Guidelines for Healthy Americans.*

United States Department of Agriculture (2005b) *My Pyramid for Kids.*

Magazines

Cooking Light (www.cookinglight.com)

Newsletters

Tufts University Health and Nutrition Letter, June 2003

Online sources

See www.drweil.com for recipes in the Healthy Kitchen section.

General Index

spaghetti 28, 41, 52, 59, 72,
    75, 82, 91
spelt 28
spices 64
spinach 19, 21, 82, 91
    nutrition 84–5
squash 19, 21, 40, 48, 49,
    52, 65
staples 62–3, 67, 69
    baking supplies 64
    canned foods 63
    frozen foods 65, 67, 69
    fruits 66
    oils 63
    refrigerated foods 65, 67
    spices 64
steak 40, 55, 68
stir fry 39, 58
strawberries 50, 66, 79
sugar 17, 34, 40, 45, 49, 52,
    56, 64, 65, 91
supper 39–41
    pot luck supper 76
    spaghetti supper 75
supplements 17, 21, 22–3
sweet potatoes 40, 54, 68

tapioca 29, 62
tapioca starch flour 64
Tartrazine 80
TBHQ 80
tef 29, 62
thiamin 22, 84, 89
tofu 45, 86
tomatoes 19, 21, 37, 51, 53,
    56, 57, 65, 67, 68
tortillas 17, 36, 37, 38, 48,
    49, 51, 67
trail mix 43
travelling 77–8
triticale 28
tuna 37, 56, 63
turkey 18, 20, 36, 37, 49,
    55, 66, 69

Ullman, R. 81
United States Department of
    Agriculture 17
US Department of Health
    and Human Services 81

vegetables 17, 19, 21, 30,
    46, 60, 61, 62, 72, 91
    nutrition 83, 85–6, 87
    shopping lists 65–6, 67–8
vinegar 30, 61, 62, 77
vitamins 17, 22–3, 46, 84,
    85, 87, 89
    supplements 22–3
    Vitamin A 46, 84–5, 90
    Vitamin B 22, 84, 86, 89
    Vitamin C 82, 85, 89, 90
    Vitamin D 22, 23, 46
    Vitamin E 82, 83, 85, 87,
        88
    Vitamin K 85, 86, 87

waffles 33, 43, 47, 54, 65,
    96
walnuts 63, 82, 83
water 17, 36, 37, 37, 40, 47,
    49, 50, 71
    water balance 84, 85, 88,
        89, 90
Weiss, B. 80
wheat 22, 24, 28, 30, 45, 61

Yellow #5 79
yogurt 25, 26

Index of Recipes